How Did Jesus Know He Was God?

*Self-Consciousness and Human Knowledge of
Christ: Maritain, Rahner, and Weinandy*

William Chami

WIPF & STOCK · Eugene, Oregon

HOW DID JESUS KNOW HE WAS GOD?
Self-Consciousness and Human Knowledge of Christ:
Maritain, Rahner, and Weinandy

Wipf & Stock
An Imprint of Wipf and Stock Publishers
199 W. 8th Ave., Suite 3
Eugene, OR 97401

www.wipfandstock.com

PAPERBACK ISBN: 978-1-7252-6060-3
HARDCOVER ISBN: 978-1-7252-6059-7
EBOOK ISBN: 978-1-7252-6061-0

Manufactured in the U.S.A.   MARCH 12, 2020

Contents

Contents

Introduction

BORN OUT OF THE questions concerning the historical activity and subjectivity of Jesus of Nazareth, the self-consciousness of Christ has proven to be a significant theological issue, especially within the last few centuries of christological reflection. The issue at hand primarily concerns how the divine Son becomes humanly conscious of himself as the divine Son. That is, how does Jesus, in his human mind and self-consciousness, come to know himself as divine, and so come to know the Father's will for him throughout his life?[1] To a contemporary reader, such an investigation may seem excessively abstract. One may wonder how this esoteric question bears any relevance to the faith of everyday Catholics. Furthermore, some may genuinely ask whether an adequate answer can be found since the psychological function of individuals, especially that of the Son of God made man, cannot be fully entered into through the tools of philosophical and theological inquiry. With these concerns in mind, it must be said that although we are unable to know the innermost depths of

---

1. Such a consideration emerged following the Council of Chalcedon and is first embodied in the epistle of St. Fulgentius of Ruspe (c. 468–533) to Ferrandus who explores the awareness of the divinity as present to the human soul of Christ, see Fulgentius, *Epistola XIV* 31 (PL 65: 420–21).

1

Jesus' human mind, this does not mean that we cannot say
anything about the present subject. After all, the dangers of
both an extreme rationalism and an excessive fideism must
be avoided in order to make an attempt at a competent
christological investigation.[2]

The present question, despite being shrouded in
mystery and considered by some as overly abstract
or irrelevant, is significant nonetheless.[3] It is a vital
component of the Catholic faith as it primarily concerns
the importance of Jesus' role as the communicator and
revealer of divine truth. Jesus comes to reveal divine truth
so that men may have the fullness of life both in this life
and the next (John 4:14; 6:40; 10:10). The purpose of
the Incarnation, then, is the proclamation of God's love,
embodied through the words and actions of Jesus Christ.
As a result of this, Jesus possesses a unique identity as not
only the Son of the Father but also as the revealer of the
Father's love. However, the ability to reveal presupposes

2. The words of Raymond Moloney, SJ, are worthy of reflection
here: "What was in the mind and heart of Christ, and how he viewed
the world and its history, will always remain matters shrouded in the
mystery which the Son of God is in his very being. At the same time,
given that we have some objective knowledge about him, in so far as
he is both true God and true human being, given also the manifold
data of the New Testament about him, it seems that, by combining
scripture and tradition, a few statements can be made as to his
knowledge and consciousness with some degree of confidence," see
Moloney, *Knowledge of Christ*, 5–6.

3. Concerning the importance of the present question, the
International Theological Commission, in its document "The
Consciousness of Christ concerning Himself and His Mission," states:
"It is clear, then, that the Church attaches maximum importance to
the problem of the awareness (consciousness) and human knowledge
of Jesus. We are not dealing with mere theological speculations but
with the very foundation of the method and mission of the Church in
all its intimacy," see Sharkey, *ITC: Texts and Documents*, 306.

the possession of knowledge. One cannot reveal that which they do not know. It is therefore imperative that Jesus knows who he is as the Son of God, as well as what the Father wills for him, so that he may properly fulfill his role as the revealer of the Father. It seems an untenable position that the one who is entrusted to reveal divine truth should err in his comprehension and communication of that truth.[4] It is thus presupposed within this paper that while on earth, Jesus possessed evidential certitude of his identity and mission in order to effectively communicate the message of salvation to the world. As a result of this conviction, this work does not engage with the idea that the earthly Christ exhibited faith, a popular notion that has emerged in recent years.[5] One is reminded here of the apt remark of Bernard Lonergan, SJ, who states that "when everyone believes and no one knows, no one is believing reasonably."[6]

4. Leeming, "Human Knowledge of Christ," 252. Of this, Reginald Garrigou-Lagrange, OP, states: "Jesus' mission is that of the Teacher of humanity, charged with leading it to eternal life. . . . Must not the perfect Master, then, possess the evidence of what He is teaching, especially if He is Himself 'the way, the truth, and the life'? The great Sower of truth, charged with telling all human generations until the end of time 'the words of eternal life,' must have known this eternal life even while He was still on earth," see Garrigou-Lagrange, *Our Saviour and His Love for Us*, 167.

5. The notification of the Congregation for the Doctrine of the Faith on the work of Jon Sobrino, SJ, indicates the conviction of this paper: "Jesus, the Incarnate Son of God, enjoys an intimate and immediate knowledge of his Father, a 'vision' that certainly goes beyond the vision of faith. The hypostatic union and Jesus' mission of revelation and redemption require the vision of the Father and the knowledge of his plan of salvation," see CDF, *On the Works of Father Jon Sobrino SJ*, sec. 8.

6. Lonergan, *The Incarnate Word*, 675.

With regard to other preliminary clarifications, it is to be noted that this thesis, although touching upon the evidence of Scripture, is not intended to be a work of biblical exegesis. The prime aim of this work is to lay out the historical convictions surrounding this issue and elucidate the thoughts of various authors on this topic. It must also be advised that, within this thesis, the historical councils of the Church, most specifically Chalcedon, are taken as dogmatic and binding. Finally, it is also understood that while there are a number of legitimate ways to read Scripture, this paper assumes the historicity of the scriptural accounts and aims to utilize them as valid historical indications of the life and knowledge of Jesus.

It has been traditionally maintained in Catholic theology that Jesus knew that he was God in his human mind through his possession of the beatific vision. This idea has fallen victim to considerable skepticism in recent years with many authors attempting to put forward different ideas of the kind of "vision" that Jesus possessed. Embodied within the context of this paper are the works of three main authors, Jacques Maritain, Karl Rahner, SJ, and Thomas Weinandy, OFM Cap., who, although all affirming that Jesus had certitude of his divine identity through a graced vision, disagree about the nature of this vision.[7] This paper, then, aims to elucidate these authors' conceptions about the vision of the Incarnate Christ which stood as the condition for his human self-awareness as the Son of God.

---

7. Rahner notes that "[t]he Church's doctrinal pronouncements command us to hold fast to the direct vision of the Logos by the human soul of Jesus. They do not, however, give us any theological instructions as to what precise concept of this vision of God we must hold," see Rahner, "Dogmatic Reflections," 213.

It is also understood that the vision which Jesus possesses necessarily entails certain secondary objects of knowledge that inform the Son made man about various aspects of reality. This paper is concerned with two main objects of knowledge. The first is whether the Son had an intimate knowledge of all men and women, to the extent that it can be proclaimed with St. Paul that the Son "loved me and gave himself for me" (Gal 2:20).[8] The second is whether Christ was truly ignorant about the eschatological end of the world, as suggested by his statement that "no one knows [the day and hour], not even the angels in heaven, nor the Son, but only the Father" (Mark 13:32; Matt 24:36). In explicating the views of Maritain, Rahner, and Weinandy on the vision of Christ, an attempt will be made to identify their various theological and philosophical presuppositions, their secondary objects of knowledge, and some criticisms that have been made about their works. Derived from this, an idea will be proposed in the final section of the paper on how the vision of Christ should be conceived as well as the degree to which Christ's human knowledge extended as a result of this vision.

The Traditional Consensus

The first known author to explicitly attribute the beatific vision to the Incarnate Christ is the ninth-century writer, Candide.[9] The idea that Christ possessed the beatific vision

8. Translations from Scripture are taken from the Revised Standard Version.

9. Candide, *Epistola* 6–7 (PL 106: 106). St. Fulgentius seems to express this opinion in a somewhat less explicit manner, stating: "It is very difficult and quite irreconcilable with the integrity of the Faith to assume that Christ's soul did not possess a full knowledge of its divinity, with which, according to the Faith, it physically

really took off in the period of the scholastics when it was endorsed by various noteworthy proponents, including Hugh of St. Victor,[10] Peter Lombard,[11] and most notably, St. Thomas Aquinas.[12] From here, a general consensus was formed among the theologians of the twelfth and thirteenth centuries that during his life on earth, Jesus saw God face to face through the beatific vision. Theologians from different schools of thought, whether Thomists, Scotists, Nominalists, Molinists, Augustinians, or Realists, were all in agreement that Christ as man possessed the vision of God.[13] Even the heretics of the day, including Wycliffe, Huss, Hooker, and the Jansenists, agreed with this assessment.[14] This doctrine was so firmly fixed in the minds of the scholastics that there was no room for alternative opinions. Bernard Leeming, SJ, presents the evidence concisely:

> They [the theologians] agree, moreover, that the matter is not open to discussion: 'it is part of the faith' (Toletus), 'the contrary would practically be heresy' (Petavius, the Salamanca theologians,

possesses one person," see Ott, *Fundamentals of Catholic Dogma,* 163; Fulgentius, *Epistola XIV* 26 (PL 65: 415–16).

10. Hugh of St. Victor, *De Sacramentis Christianae Fidei* 2.1.6 (PL 176: 388D–89B).

11. Lombard, *Sententiarum Libri Quatuor*, III, d. 14, n. 2 (PL 192: 783–84).

12. Aquinas, *Summa Theologica,* III, q. 9, a. 2; III, q. 10, aa. 1, 4.

13. Leeming, "Human Knowledge of Christ," 235. Garrigou-Lagrange confirms this, stating: "It is no slight matter that on this point all theologians agree, whether they be Thomists, Scotists, Suarezians, or Molinists. Their disagreement on controversial matters shows the value of their agreement on those that are not controversial," see Garrigou-Lagrange, *Our Saviour and His Love for Us,* 162, footnote 83.

14. Leeming, "Human Knowledge of Christ," 235.

Janssens), 'theologically certain' (Medina, Pesch, Lercher, Lépicier), 'the contrary would be erroneous, or rash, or unsound in faith' (Suarez, Alvarez, Platin, Billuart, Lugo, Hurter), 'taught as certain in all Catholic schools' (Galtier), 'common and certain in theology' (Solano); Stentrup sums it up: 'No Catholic theologian has a right to depart from this doctrine which touches the faith, and which has been received by the unanimous and constant agreement of approved theologians and writers.'[15]

This consensus continued until the time of the twentieth century. Garrigou-Lagrange confirms the harmony present among theologians in regard to this doctrine, stating: "The theologians answer in unison: Jesus saw what He taught in the light of the beatific vision.... This has been the common teaching of theologians particularly since the twelfth century, and the Church has declared that it would be rash to deny it."[16] Garrigou-Lagrange is here referring to the decree of the Holy Office on June 5, 1918, which stated in its propositions that it was unsafe to teach that Christ did not possess the beatific vision, while also declaring it unsafe to teach that Jesus possessed ignorance throughout his life.[17] These pronouncements enjoyed endorsement even from the Church's ordinary magisterium. Recourse to the beatific vision of Christ can be seen in Pope Pius XII's *Mystici Corporis Christi* (1943), where it is stated that Jesus began to enjoy the beatific

15. Leeming, "Human Knowledge of Christ," 235.

16. Garrigou-Lagrange, *Our Saviour and His Love for Us*, 162.

17. Denzinger et al., *Compendium*, 3645–47. See also the decree of the Holy Office on July 3, 1907, *Lamentabili*, which condemned both the ascription of error to Christ as well as the gradual unfolding of his messianic awareness, see Denzinger et al., *Compendium*, 3433, 3435.

vision from the moment of his conception, with all the members of his mystical body being present to him at all times.[18] Further reference from Pius XII can be seen in his later encyclical, *Haurietis Aquas* (1956), where he confirms the existence of both beatific knowledge and infused science in the soul of Christ.[19] Jean Galot, SJ, has argued that the notion of Christ's beatific vision was maintained so ardently by the Church as a defense against the claims of the Modernists in the nineteenth and twentieth centuries who denied that Jesus was aware of his divinity.[20] In the opinion of Galot, the beatific vision served to safeguard Christ's identity as true comprehensor, having extensive knowledge of himself as God and of his mission. This is why the Church considered the departure from this traditional doctrine as an unsafe theological opinion.[21]

18. Pius XII, *Mystici Corporis Christi,* sec. 75.

19. Pius XII, *Haurietis Aquas,* sec. 56.

20. Galot, *Who is Christ?,* 357–58, footnote 33.

21. Galot insists that the decree of the Holy Office did not confirm doctrine, but was rather born out of reaction against certain theories which sought to undermine Christ's role as knower: "One cannot attribute an unduly absolute value to these decrees, born of a defensive reaction against certain theories; and it is important to distinguish between the truth of faith that they sought to preserve and that must be maintained, and the private opinions of scholastic theory that do not possess the same degree of certitude," see Galot, *Who is Christ?,* 357–58, footnote 33. Jacques Dupuis, SJ, argues similarly that the declarations of the Holy Office 1918, and even that of Pius XII's *Mystici Corporis Christi,* are only disciplinary rather than doctrinal, see Dupuis, *Who Do You Say I Am?,* 121–22. Moloney affirms this idea, writing that these declarations "should be related to the climate of fear and confusion brought about by modernism itself. . . . [T]he reaction of those in authority was the prudential one of reinforcing the safe theories of the past, but it is important to underline that the intervention of the magisterium did not invoke the ultimate note of irreformable doctrine," see Moloney, *Knowledge of Christ,* 119–20.

Shift in the Theological Pendulum

Despite the idea of Jesus possessing the beatific vision receiving notable support from the Catholic theological tradition, at the time of the early twentieth century, the theological consensus that had been maintained by theologians for so long began to slowly sway in new directions. Indeed, it is not today uncommon to find theologians who outright oppose this idea, opting instead for other theories that explain how Jesus knew himself as God in his human mind. Alternative theories offered include a kind of mission-consciousness (Balthasar), unobjectified filial consciousness (Rahner, Weinandy), "abba experience" (Schillebeeckx), and an infused prophetic insight existing with authentic human knowledge of the Father (Galot).[22] The reason for this shift in consensus seems to derive itself from a modern interest in Jesus as a "real" historical subject. In an age of emerging interest in the historical subjectivity and psychology of the historical Jesus of Nazareth, first-century Palestinian Jew, some theologians have moved away from the traditional consensus in a seeming attempt to make Christ's psyche, as it was exercised in its historical conditions, more "credible." As Jeremy Wilkins observes: "Beatific knowledge seems to preclude concrete historical subjectivity."[23] It is being wondered how Christ could have been culturally conditioned by his historical milieu if he possessed from the moment of his conception the vision of the divine essence.[24] Moreover, it is sometimes asked whether beatific knowledge is compatible with the suffering, temptation, ignorance, and kenosis of

---

22. Wilkins, "Love and Knowledge of God," 83–84.

23. Wilkins, "Love and Knowledge of God," 84.

24. Wilkins, "Love and Knowledge of God," 84.

Christ that is commonly portrayed throughout Scripture. The turning away from the traditional consensus then may be described as a shift from a "Christology from above" to a "Christology from below." In the former, as especially prevalent during the neo-scholastic revival of the nineteenth and twentieth centuries, the beatific vision was posited as a necessary consequence of the fact that Jesus was God. For theologians today who aspire to work within the parameters of a "Christology from below," the approach is inverted. They contend that it is because Jesus is human that he cannot possess the beatific vision, as its possession is an impediment to his concrete existential subjectivity as a real historical figure. In this way, the current modern approach seems to concern itself with upholding the humanity and historical activity of Jesus as opposed to emphasizing his transcendent nature as the Logos.[25]

It can also be argued that the transition away from the old consensus finds its roots in the renewal of Catholic theology in the middle of the twentieth century. Emerging out of Leo XIII's encyclical *Aeterni Patris* (1879), the domination of neo-scholastic theology came to a close at the Second Vatican Council. As new theological methods emerged following Vatican II, so did new ways of tackling on Christ's knowledge and historical subjectivity. This judgment seems to be affirmed by Leeming, who states:

> There were, indeed, in the nineteenth century and the beginning of this, a few dissentient voices among Catholic theologians. But they served as exceptions who proved the rule. Generally, they explicitly said they rejected the whole 'scholastic' tradition and outlook upon the matter, and

25. White, "Dyotheletism and the Instrumental Human Consciousness of Jesus," 397.

took as their norm nothing save Scripture and the earlier Fathers.[26]

This theological "turning of the tide" is reflected in the convictions of various modern theologians who view the old thesis of Jesus' beatific vision as resulting in some kind of quasi-Docetism. Rahner argues that "[s]uch statements sound almost mythological today when one first hears them; they seem to be contrary to the real humanity and historical nature of Our Lord,"[27] while Gerald O'Collins, SJ, and Daniel Kendall, SJ, write that "[f]or many people it would seem to inject a strong element of make-believe into the whole of his life story and cast doubt on his authentic humanity."[28] Even the International Theological Commission has shown little resistance against the current winds of change. In its three most recent documents on Christology, "Select Questions on Christology" (1979), "Theology, Christology and Anthropology" (1981), and especially, "The Consciousness of Christ concerning Himself and His mission" (1985), not once had Jesus' beatific vision been mentioned. Although these documents produced by the International Theological Commission do not possess the same authority as the magisterium of the Church, the omission of Jesus' beatific vision from its recent documents does shed considerable light on how far the theological pendulum has swung. It seems that the Commission has left ample room open for new theories concerning Christ's self-consciousness and human knowledge that do not directly involve the traditional doctrine of the beatific vision.

26. Leeming, "Human Knowledge of Christ," 235–36.
27. Rahner, "Dogmatic Reflections," 194–95.
28. O'Collins and Kendall, "The Faith of Jesus," 409.

Consciousness and Human Knowledge

Before we can continue, it is necessary to elucidate the notions of "consciousness" and "human knowledge" as used within the title of this paper. Despite being related in some ways, these two notions are fundamentally distinct as they pertain to different facets of reality. Human knowledge refers to the process by which individuals, through their objective conceptualization of reality, come to know objects through the process of understanding and judgment.[29] A treatment of Jesus' human knowledge, however, is altogether different from a treatment of his self-consciousness. Regarding consciousness, it must first be admitted that there is no harmonious agreement among scholars in regard to its definition.[30] It is a relatively new concept, with the research undertaken in recent years on consciousness remaining quite preliminary and undeveloped. For the purpose of this paper, Lonergan's concise definition of consciousness as "the experience of a subject as opposed to the knowledge of an object" will be adopted. However, "experience" here must be taken in the strict sense of the term, whereby it refers to a preliminary unstructured awareness of oneself and one's acts that is the foundation and prerequisite for all intellectual inquiry.[31] It is pre-reflexive because it is logically prior to objective knowing, but it is also reflexive insofar as it accompanies the act of knowing.[32]

29. Moloney, *Knowledge of Christ*, 99.

30. Moloney, *Knowledge of Christ*, 107.

31. Lonergan, *Ontological and Psychological Constitution of Christ*, 161. Lonergan believes that consciousness understood as "experience" is in concord with Catholic tradition and the *sensus fidelium*, see Lonergan, *Ontological and Psychological Constitution of Christ*, 191.

32. White, "Dyotheletism and the Instrumental Human

Though knowledge is indeed conscious, consciousness is not constituted by the subject's apprehension of objects but is rather the subject's "experiential self-awareness in the process of knowing."[33] Ultimately, it is a preliminary and unstructured awareness that reveals the subject as an experiential subject. That is, it informs us that it is we who are carrying out our conscious activity.[34] Lonergan states:

> [W]e are conscious because we are actually sensing, understanding, judging, choosing; and it does not matter at all what the object is that is sensed, understood, judged, chosen. . . . For consciousness belongs to the one sensing, understanding, judging, choosing, and reflecting, and is always on the side of the subject who senses, understands, judges, chooses, reflects.[35]

It must be said that the vision that Jesus possesses is not itself a form of consciousness. In order to perceive the vision, Jesus must be conscious in the first place.[36] The

Consciousness of Jesus," 416–17.

33. White, "Dyotheletism and the Instrumental Human Consciousness of Jesus," 416.

34. Moloney, *Knowledge of Christ*, 109.

35. Lonergan, *Ontological and Psychological Constitution of Christ*, 195.

36. Moloney writes that "our Lord's awareness of his own nature as a divine nature is not exactly a matter of consciousness, in Lonergan's narrow sense of that term, but is a result of a combination of consciousness and of Christ's direct vision of the divinity. Through human consciousness one might, as in the case of Christ, be conscious of a divine person, but not of the divine nature, since it was a divine person who became incarnate, not a divine nature. . . . This grasp of the divinity by the man Jesus is an act of knowledge requiring the immediate vision of God; but it also requires his own human consciousness if he is to grasp it as *his* divinity" (emphasis original), see Moloney, *Knowledge of Christ*, 100–101. See also Lonergan, *Ontological and Psychological Constitution of Christ*, 205.

vision, rather, serves as an intellectual grace that informs the Son or makes him conscious of his divine identity. Although there are difficulties associated with the use of the term "self-consciousness," the term has been retained for the most part in academic works by theologians and philosophers to denote Christ's self-awareness of himself as a divine person. In the same manner, this term will be employed throughout this thesis as a reference to the self-awareness of the Son with regard to his own divine personhood. Therefore, when the term "self-consciousness" is used, it is referring to the Son's apprehension of himself as a divine person while the term "human knowledge" refers to the Son's knowledge of particular objects. In explicating these preliminary considerations, we are now in a better position to present the works of our three main authors.

I. Jacques Maritain

THOMIST PHILOSOPHER JACQUES MARITAIN, in his 1967 publication *De la Grâce et de l'humanité de Jésus*, presented his thoughts on the issue of Jesus' self-consciousness and his human knowledge. Like any good Thomist, Maritain's ideas were built on the long-established foundations set by St. Thomas Aquinas and virtually the whole Catholic theological tradition which maintained that the Incarnate Christ, during his life on earth, possessed the beatific vision.[1] More than this, it was also postulated that Jesus possessed two other forms of human knowledge: infused science as the most perfect of the prophets, and acquired knowledge such as we possess.[2] It was said that Jesus ob-

1. For St. Thomas, Jesus' possession of the beatific vision was soteriological in function, that is, the Incarnate Son possessed what he himself had come to give us, see Aquinas, *Summa Theologica*, III, q. 9, a. 2. For a defense on this reading of St. Thomas, see Mansini, "Understanding St. Thomas on Christ's Immediate Knowledge of God," 93–96.

2. For St. Thomas's treatment of Jesus' threefold human knowledge, see Aquinas, *Summa Theologica*, III, qq. 9–12. Although the idea that Jesus learned experientially was initially denied by St. Thomas, he would later recant his previous repudiation of this idea and affirm that Jesus did indeed learn through experience: "And hence, although I wrote differently (III, *Sent.* D, xiv, A. 3; D, xviii, A. 3), it must be said that in Christ there was acquired knowledge," see

tained knowledge experientially throughout his life on account of his true humanity, while the beatific vision and infused science were interpreted as graces given to the Incarnate Son for the purpose of his soteriological mission.[3] This idea of the threefold structure of Jesus' human knowledge dominated the Catholic theological scene for centuries. As will be demonstrated in this chapter, Maritain's thesis was significant in reinforcing the traditional notions of Jesus' beatific vision and infused science as the condition for Christ's self-awareness as the Son of God. More than this, Maritain, through his distinctions in consciousness, was able to develop these traditional concepts so as to better articulate how it is that Jesus, in his historical life, could be *simul viator et comprehensor* ("at once wayfarer and beholder").[4] For the purpose of this chapter, Maritain's treatment of Christ's beatific vision and infused science will be presented, as well as how these two forms of graced knowledge participate in one another so as to produce in the Son the knowledge of his own divine identity and mission.

Preliminary Remarks and Methodology

As previously stated, Maritain's work relied heavily upon the thought of St. Thomas. This does not mean that Maritain's thesis was a mere monotonous expression of what had previously been argued by the Angelic Doctor. Rather,

---

Aquinas, *Summa Theologica*, III, q. 9, a. 4, co. It has been argued by many scholars that St. Thomas was the first medieval theologian to advance the notion of acquired knowledge in Christ, see Madigan, "Did Jesus 'Progress in Wisdom'?," 180.

3. White, "Infused Science of Christ," 617.

4. See Aquinas, *Summa Theologica*, III, q. 15, a. 10.

I. Jacques Maritain

Maritain took St. Thomas's notions of Jesus' beatific vision and infused science and developed them successfully through his ingenious distinction of the different levels of consciousness that exist in the Incarnate Son. For example, Maritain argued that the human soul of Jesus possessed consciousness not only as it is common to our own human experience, which he refers to as the "here-below" of Christ's soul but, further than this, a "supraconscious of the Spirit."[5] In substantiating the existence of this "supraconscious of the Spirit," Maritain argues that its properties are analogous to the unconscious functioning of the agent intellect and that this supraconscious was present even in the minds of the ancients, in particular, in Aristotle when he spoke on "inspirations."[6] The supraconscious, as with the subconscious, is the negatively established category for denoting that which is not conscious,[7] while the "here-below" region of Christ's soul is rendered akin to the ordinary human consciousness that functions in ourselves and in which lays present unconscious tendencies, instincts, and sensations, as well as the agent intellect and will.[8] This distinction between supraconsciousness and lower consciousness is a central premise in Maritain's thesis, one that helped him to convey how it is that Jesus could be both wayfarer and beholder at the same time. He argues that in the supraconscious region of his soul, Jesus was the perfect comprehensor, while in his lower consciousness, Jesus

5. The "here-below" of Christ's soul is also referred to as "lower consciousness" and "wayfaring consciousness" herein. It is also worth noting that Maritain refers to the supraconscious region as the "heaven" of Christ's soul.

6. Maritain, *Grace and Humanity*, 49.

7. Maritain, *Grace and Humanity*, 49, footnote 2.

8. Maritain, *Grace and Humanity*, 55.

served as a wayfarer.[9] Maritain further explains that there exists a certain level of incommunicability between these two spheres of consciousness. The content present in the supraconscious region is inaccessible to lower consciousness, and so cannot pass into it except by "mode of general influx, and of comforting, and of participated light."[10] As Romanus Cessario describes, the content of the supraconscious present to Jesus-comprehensor cannot and does not "inform" Jesus-viator in his wayfaring consciousness, but instead serves only as an illuminating light.[11]

An example of the way in which Maritain employs this distinction concerns the statement made by St. Luke that Jesus "increased in wisdom and in stature, and in favor with God and man" (Luke 2:52). Maritain recognizes that this passage of St. Luke appears to conflict with the words of St. John which describe Jesus as "full of grace and truth" (John 1:14). Herein lies the apparent contrariety, since St. Luke seems to describe a continual increase in wisdom and grace throughout the life of Jesus, whereas St. John seems to think that Jesus was filled with both grace and truth to the utmost degree. This is where Maritain's distinction between supraconsciousness and wayfaring consciousness is made useful. According to Maritain, since St. Thomas lacked the distinction between supraconsciousness and wayfaring consciousness that Maritain himself employs,

9. Of this distinction, Maritain states: "If one does not admit in the soul of Christ a difference of level, a *heaven* of the soul, but supraconscious, for the state of *comprehensor*, and a *here-below* of the soul, the here-below of consciousness and of the conscious and deliberate operations, for the state of *viator*, I believe that one is inevitably led to wrong the one or the other of these two states" (emphasis original), see Maritain, *Grace and Humanity,* 59.

10. Maritain, *Grace and Humanity,* 59.

11. Cessario, "Incarnate Wisdom," 339–40.

St. Thomas was not able to resolve these two seemingly conflicting texts and so, in his answer, did not do justice to the declaration of St. Luke.[12] Maritain, on the other hand, was able to harmoniously integrate both statements of St. John and St. Luke into the reality of Christ's life by stating that Jesus was indeed maximally filled with both grace and truth as per St. John, but only in the supraconscious region of his soul where he functioned as comprehensor. However, because this region is largely inaccessible to his lower consciousness, Jesus also, at the same time, grew in grace and truth, but only in his lower consciousness where he was viator.[13] Both wisdom and grace increased in Jesus, but they did so only in one part of his soul, while in the other part it was had perfectly, as St. Thomas renders. This method of distinction was both innovative and useful in delineating Jesus' role as both comprehensor and viator and is, as will be demonstrated, consistent with the rest of Maritain's treatment on the whole question of Jesus' self-consciousness and human knowledge.

Beatific Vision and Infused Science in Christ

Maritain holds that Jesus, from the moment of his conception, possessed the beatific vision.[14] Maritain's affirmation of the beatific vision in the Incarnate Son is predicated on Jesus' role as comprehensor and on the nature of the hypostatic union. He argues that because it is the Word that

12. St. Thomas asserted that Jesus could not increase in grace, see Aquinas, *Summa Theologica*, III, q. 7, a. 12, a statement which seems to favor St. John's assertion over and above that of St. Luke's, see Maritain, *Grace and Humanity*, 50, footnote 3.

13. Maritain, *Grace and Humanity*, 76.

14. Maritain, *Grace and Humanity*, 89.

is Incarnate and so subsists in human nature, it is necessary that this assumed human nature "participate in the Deity to the sovereign degree possible, in short, that it be elevated to the state of comprehensor, that is to say, that it see God."[15] Maritain's attribution of the beatific vision to the Incarnate Son, then, seems to derive itself from a so-called "principle of perfection," that is to say that since the human nature is hypostatically united to the divine person, the humanity is thus conferred with perfect human attributes, among these the beatific vision.[16] Furthermore, because Jesus was comprehensor only in the supraconscious region of his soul, the beatific vision only occurred in and was confined to that region. It did not penetrate and permeate his lower consciousness unreservedly, except by mode of general influence and participated light.[17] This means that the beatific vision did not produce in Jesus the complementary perfection, beatitude, and glory that is connatural to the vision.[18] More than this, because there existed a partition between the supraconscious region and lower consciousness, the human actions of Jesus were not

15. Maritain, *Grace and Humanity*, 69.

16. For a helpful outline on the so-called "principle of perfection," see White, "Voluntary Action of the Earthly Christ," 500. Although St. Thomas argued that Jesus' possession of the beatific vision derived itself from a principle of economy as opposed to a principle of metaphysical necessity deduced from the fact of the hypostatic union, he does indeed make mention of this principle of perfection as present in Christ's knowledge, see Aquinas, *Summa Theologica*, III, q. 9, aa. 1, 2, 4; III, q. 11, a. 1; III, q. 12, a. 1. St. Thomas also writes that "the nearer any recipient is to an inflowing cause, the more does it partake of its influence," see Aquinas, *Summa Theologica*, III, q. 7, a. 1, co.

17. Maritain, *Grace and Humanity*, 23.

18. This is the distinguishing factor between Jesus' beatific vision and the beatific vision of the blessed in heaven, since the vision did not produce in Jesus its natural consequences of beatitude and glory, see Maritain, *Grace and Humanity*, 85–86.

led by the beatific vision, but were rather predicated on the Son's rational powers. Maritain states: "It [the beatific vision] did not beatify the soul of Christ and all its powers. It was not the immediate rule and the determining principle of all the action of Christ and of all the operations of His soul."[19]

Through the beatific vision, Jesus knew that he was God in a manner most perfect. This is because Jesus saw in the vision the Holy Trinity and consequently himself as the divine Word.[20] This knowledge was also perfect to excess and did not increase in the richness of objective content over time.[21] However, because this vision was only present in the supraconscious region of his soul, its contents were inaccessible to Christ's lower consciousness where he functioned as viator. In addition to this, because the beatific vision is "an eternal flash of which absolutely nothing can be said through an idea," it was impossible for Jesus to express to his audience the content present to him in the beatific vision.[22] That is to say, it is an altogether

19. Maritain, *Grace and Humanity*, 24. The beatific vision "did not invade and did not glorify the entire soul, and did not replace the reason as immediate rule of the actions of the soul, in short which created in the heights of the soul a sort of closed heaven," see Maritain, *Grace and Humanity*, 94. Such a distinction was also utilized by St. Thomas, who argued that the vision left unaffected the corporeal and sensate faculties of Jesus, see Aquinas, *Summa Theologica*, III, q. 46, aa. 6–8; White, "Infused Science of Christ," 636. This is to be contrasted with the resurrection whereby the beatific vision began to permeate the entire soul of Christ so as to produce beatitude and glory, even in his human faculties, see Maritain, *Grace and Humanity*, 24; Aquinas, *Summa Theologica*, III, q. 54, a. 3.

20. Maritain, *Grace and Humanity*, 56.

21. Maritain, *Grace and Humanity*, 107.

22. Maritain, *Grace and Humanity*, 97. Maritain further states that "there is *absolutely no possibility of expressing through concepts, neither to others or to oneself, that which is known through the*

unthematic and simple vision, one that is ineffable in essence and inaccessible to Jesus-viator.[23] Hence it was impossible for Jesus, in his state as wayfarer, to "make use" of the vision and its contents.[24] Although Jesus, in his state as comprehensor, knew that he was God through the beatific vision, the vision could not, in its unadulterated form, inform Jesus-viator of his divine identity. It was necessary, then, that Jesus possess another type of special knowledge in his wayfaring consciousness so as to apprehend his divine identity and communicate this truth to others.

From the creation of his soul, Jesus also possessed infused science.[25] This was attributed to Christ traditionally by virtue of the fact that he is the most perfect of the prophets. However, his possession of infused science differed from the prophets of old in both

Vision" (emphasis original), see Maritain, *Grace and Humanity*, 60. John McDermott, SJ, argues that St. Thomas did not consider the vision to be unthematic in exactly the same way that Maritain does, see McDermott, "How Did Jesus Know He Was God?," 284.

23. As Cessario explains: "If we affirm that Christ possessed the beatific vision during his earthly life, we do not therefore maintain that the beatific vision directly influenced his daily life. The beatific vision remains paralyzing, and no creature can act as a result of it," see Cessario, "Incarnate Wisdom," 338. Thomas Joseph White, OP, affirms this notion, writing that "the vision of God is not conceptual or notional, but immediate and intuitive. Consequently, it cannot be 'assimilated' by Christ's habitual, conceptual manner of knowing and willing in any direct fashion," see White, "Voluntary Action of the Earthly Christ," 516.

24. Maritain writes that Jesus "knew certainly, and in the most perfect manner, His divinity through the Beatific Vision, but this Vision was shut up in the supraconscious paradise of His soul, and, moreover, it was by essence absolutely simple and absolutely *inexpressible* in any idea" (emphasis original), see Maritain, *Grace and Humanity*, 107.

25. Maritain, *Grace and Humanity*, 90.

degree and habit.[26] St. Thomas classically asserted that the scope of Jesus' infused science extended to all that can be known by man in potency, but was in act with respect to the things that must have been known by Jesus for the purpose of his soteriological mission.[27] St. Thomas also held that the infused science was infinite in perfection and devoid of any growth. As a consequence of this, the infused science of Jesus extended to the knowledge of all singulars, past, present, and future, from the moment that his soul was created.[28] This proximate power to know all things in infancy seemed, at least to Maritain, difficult to reconcile with the demands of Jesus as true man and viator, and incompatible with the "mode connatural to the human soul" that St. Thomas himself admits.[29] Despite his quarrels with this doctrine of St. Thomas, Maritain chose not to reject this assertion outright. Instead, through his distinction between the supraconscious and wayfaring consciousness, Maritain was able to affirm this idea of St. Thomas that the infused science was infinite in order and without growth while, at the same time, claiming that there existed another state of infused science in the soul of Christ that was both finite and increasing in time.[30] He

26. For a concise explanation of this distinction, see White, "Infused Science of Christ," 629–30.

27. Aquinas, *Summa Theologica*, III, q. 11, a. 5, obj. 2, co., ad. 2; White, "Voluntary Action of the Earthly Christ," 531–32, footnote 68.

28. Aquinas, *Summa Theologica*, III, q. 11, a. 1, obj. 3, co., ad. 3. Nevertheless, there is a distinction to be made between Jesus' potential to know all things in his infused science as an infant and the inability of the infant Jesus to willfully actualize this infused insight, see Maritain, *Grace and Humanity*, 92.

29. Maritain, *Grace and Humanity*, 93.

30. The way in which this infused science experienced growth was in accord with Jesus' growing need for it. Maritain states that "at each moment of this development it extended itself to all that which

states that in the supraconscious region of his soul, Jesus possessed not only the beatific vision but also an infused science that extended to all things absolutely and which did not grow over the course of his life.[31] However, because this infused science was present only in his supraconscious and to his state as comprehensor, it could neither penetrate his lower consciousness nor itself be expressed in human mode.[32] It was thus necessary that Jesus possess another form of infused science for his state as wayfarer. Maritain writes:

> In order that Christ as viator might express to Himself, *say* to Himself, in His consciousness of man like unto us . . . it was necessary that this infused science not find itself only in the supra-conscious paradise of the soul of Christ; it was necessary also that, in proportion as the sphere of the consciousness or of the here-below of the soul of Christ forms itself, His infused science hold sway in this other sphere . . . [I]n order that Christ could make use of it during His earthly life, *in the sphere of the here-below of the soul of Christ*, where . . . it found itself *under the state of way*.[33]

Jesus had need to know *at that moment* (I mean at that period of His progress in age and in wisdom)" (emphasis original), see Maritain, *Grace and Humanity*, 96.

31. Maritain, *Grace and Humanity*, 94.

32. Like the beatific vision, the infinite infused science began to permeate the entire soul of Christ only after the resurrection and made all things explicitly known to him in order that he may exercise his role as universal Lord, expressing decrees, judgments, and commandments in heaven, see Maritain, *Grace and Humanity*, 96–97, footnote 15.

33. Maritain, *Grace and Humanity*, 94–95 (emphasis original).

I. Jacques Maritain

According to Maritain, the infused science of Christ found itself under two states: in one state that was maximally perfect but incommunicable for Jesus-comprehensor, and in another state that was finite in order and yet expressible for Jesus-viator. It must be stated, however, that the infused science found in his wayfaring consciousness was not enough to provide Jesus-viator with certitude of his identity as the Son of God. This is because infused science, even in its most elevated form, lacks immediate evidence and as such must be accepted in faith.[34] This can be contrasted with the beatific vision which, being immediate knowledge, would allow the Incarnate Son to apprehend intuitively and *with certitude* his identity as the Son of God.[35] However, because the beatific vision was shut up in the supraconscious region of Christ's soul, it could not serve as the condition for the self-awareness of Jesus-viator. In a similar manner, the infused science, when taken by itself, would not be enough to provide Jesus-viator with an immediate certitude that he is the Son of God since it is mediated knowledge and must necessarily be accepted in faith.[36] Hence, in order for Jesus-viator to know with certitude his divine identity, these two forms of objective knowledge must cooperate with one another. That is to say, the mediated, indirect knowledge of the infused science, as found in his wayfaring consciousness, must itself participate in the immediate,

34. White, "Infused Science of Christ," 633.

35. White, "Dyotheletism and the Instrumental Human Consciousness of Jesus," 418–19.

36. White, "Voluntary Action of the Earthly Christ," 518–19. This idea is also present in the work of Lonergan, who maintained that the only way in which the Son as man could have certitude of his own divine identity is through the immediate knowledge of the vision, see Lonergan, *Ontological and Psychological Constitution of Christ*, 265.

direct knowledge of the beatific vision, as located in the supraconscious region of his soul.

Maritain states that the "intrinsic evidence [of the infused science] was a *participation of the very evidence of the vision*."[37] This means that the intellectual knowledge of the infused science, as found under both states, was immediately ruled by the beatific vision.[38] It is explained by Maritain that because Christ came to reveal the Father, the divine mysteries, and his own divine personhood, it was thus necessary that Jesus possess the beatific vision in order that he may bear witness to these divine mysteries and reveal them to others.[39] The beatific vision stands alone as the only evidence for Christ's divinity. However, this evidence can be, and in fact is, participated in by the infused science which reveals to Jesus-viator things divine.[40] It is the vision, which is "the *actuation of His intellect by the divine essence itself in the light of glory*,"[41] that serves as the immediate rule of the infused science; a fact that is necessary to admit if one wishes to maintain that Jesus-viator had certitude of his own divine identity and mission. Maritain states that "it is this participated evidence of the Vision which gave to the infused science of the Son of God *viator* a *divinely* sovereign *certitude* with regard to all that which it knew, and especially with regard to the very divinity of Jesus."[42] Furthermore, the knowledge received from this participation was not maximally perfect from the time of his infancy, but rather continued to grow

---

37. Maritain, *Grace and Humanity,* 98 (emphasis original).

38. Maritain, *Grace and Humanity,* 101.

39. Maritain, *Grace and Humanity,* 104.

40. Maritain, *Grace and Humanity,* 104.

41. Maritain, *Grace and Humanity,* 101 (emphasis original).

42. Maritain, *Grace and Humanity,* 107 (emphasis original).

in richness and perfection all throughout his life and was
perfected at such a rate so as to give the divine child of
twelve a complete conceptual knowledge of his own divine
sonship and mission.[43]

Regarding the type of participation that occurred between the infused science and the beatific vision, Maritain
argues that the infused science served as an exchange unit,
receiving first the light of the vision and then converting its
ineffable mysteries into an expressible and communicable
species.[44] He states that "thanks to the ideative forms of the
infused science such as it found itself in the here-below
of His soul, something was rendered accessible to men,
through the means of concepts (*verba mentis*) in which the
intellect of Christ uttered."[45] That is, the infused science
bridged the chasm between the two regions of Christ's
soul and made accessible to Jesus-viator the content of the
immediate and unthematic vision.[46] It is the infused science participating in the light of the vision that allowed
Jesus to know in his wayfaring consciousness "His own
divinity, His own procession from the Father, His Incarnation, His redemptive Mission, the unity in nature of the
three divine Persons, the procession of the Holy Spirit, in
short, all the divine Inaccessible which He had to reveal,

43. Maritain, *Grace and Humanity*, 108, 118–20.

44. Maritain, *Grace and Humanity*, 102–3.

45. Maritain, *Grace and Humanity*, 103.

46. As White succinctly explains, there exists a debate between
scholars as to whether St. Thomas treated the infused science as a
necessary translator of the vision or whether he believed that Jesus
could know something about the vision through his agent intellect
and so express its contents through ordinary, acquired knowledge,
see White, "Infused Science of Christ," 636–37. It seems that one
could safely categorize Maritain in the former camp of scholars, see
Maritain, *Grace and Humanity*, 72–73.

to 'tell' to men,—*ipse enarravit.*[47] The beatific vision did not, therefore, render the infused science as superfluous. Rather the two, by nature of their intrinsic relation, were necessary for providing the Son as viator with knowledge of his divine identity as well as the divine mysteries that he came to reveal.

Secondary Objects of Knowledge

Maritain holds that in the supraconscious region of his soul, Jesus-comprehensor knew all things with maximal perfection through the beatific vision and his infinite infused science.[48] This knowledge included all the details concerning his soteriological mission, extending even to the knowledge of individual believers for whom he died.[49] In this way, Maritain was able to affirm the statements made by both St. Paul and Pius XII that, during his passion, Jesus possessed a knowledge of all individuals for whom he was saving and enveloped them with infinite redeeming charity.[50] However, in his wayfaring consciousness, Jesus-viator did not possess an exhaustive knowledge of all things but rather knew aspects of his mission in a manner that was divinely true and certain through his infused science participating in the vision, which continually grew "in the richness of objective content" over the course of his life.[51]

Concerning his treatment of the supposed ignorance of Jesus concerning the last day (Mark 13:32; Matt 24:36),

47. Maritain, *Grace and Humanity,* 104.
48. Maritain, *Grace and Humanity,* 94.
49. Maritain, *Grace and Humanity,* 89, footnote 1.
50. Gal 2:20; Pius XII, *Mystici Corporis Christi,* sec. 75.
51. Maritain, *Grace and Humanity,* 110.

Maritain argues that the final "day and hour" was indeed known by Jesus-comprehensor through the beatific vision and his infinite infused science. However, Jesus-viator did not know the "day and hour" since the information that he received through the infused science participating in the vision was not infinite as was the kind present in his supraconscious, but rather grew over time and was received by Jesus in a manner that was continually progressive.[52] Hence, as comprehensor, Jesus knew perfectly all facets of his life and mission through the beatific vision and his infinite infused science, while as viator he knew them in a progressive manner through his infused science participating in the vision and only to the extent necessary for fulfilling his role as both revealer and savior.

Criticisms

Maritain's thesis was useful in reinforcing the traditional schema of Jesus' threefold human knowledge while also helping to develop it through his differentiation between the different levels of consciousness in the Incarnate Son. Maritain's distinction between the supraconscious and wayfaring consciousness helped to explain how it is that Jesus could know with absolute certainty his own divine identity as the Son of God and his soteriological mission, while at the same time experiencing growth in knowledge throughout his life as proper to his function as wayfarer. For some, this distinction in consciousness is both commendable and resourceful in the development of a purely Thomistic Christology, one which assists in reinforcing St. Thomas's notion of Jesus as *simul viator et comprehensor*.[53]

52. Maritain, *Grace and Humanity*, 96, footnote 13.
53. Oakes, *Infinity Dwindled to Infancy*, 220–21.

However, others view this distinction as an unrealistic qualification which endangers the psychological unity of the earthly Jesus. Engelbert Gutwenger, SJ, asserts:

> The attempt to divide the human soul of Christ into different regions in order to house contradictory spiritual experiences is . . . hardly acceptable. For consciousness is an undivided and homogenous factor, at least insofar as a definite conscious experience necessarily excludes its opposite from the psychological point of view when it reaches a certain intensity. If we prefer to ignore this fact we run the risk of implying more than one *ego*.[54]

Other criticisms have been made by Galot, who considers the idea of the beatific vision in the Incarnate Son as precarious to the authenticity of his assumed humanity. It is claimed by Galot that Jesus' possession of the beatific vision would extend the scope of Jesus' human knowledge to such an extent so as to endanger the true humanity and authentic intellectual development of Jesus. Galot categorizes this danger as an epistemological Monophysitism, stating:

> This perfection attributed to Christ's knowledge is such that one no longer respects sufficiently the distinction between the divine nature and the human nature. . . . Human understanding is clothed with divine properties as regards the entire domain of knowledge. One can see

---

54. Gutwenger, "The Problem of Christ's Knowledge," 92 (emphasis original). In addition to this, McDermott has criticized Maritain's division of the intellect as harmful to an understanding of the soul as the unifying principle of the human composite, see McDermott, "How Did Jesus Know He Was God?," 284, while Moloney has argued that "divinity implies consciousness. The notion of divinity in a state of suspended consciousness is an impossible one in the Judeo-Christian tradition about God," see Moloney, *Knowledge of Christ*, 35.

immediately the risk of Monophysitism, and
more precisely the difficulty in acknowledging
the inherent limitations of human knowledge, a
necessary recognition for avoiding all confusion
with the perfection of divine knowledge.[55]

Perhaps the most forceful criticism advanced against
Christ's beatific vision concerns the compatibility between
the suffering of Jesus, embodied by his time on the cross
and finding its climax at the cry of dereliction, and the
beatific joy that is experienced in and is connatural to
the vision. Such an objection has been echoed by notable
theologians such as Balthasar, Rahner, and Gutwenger,
who each maintain that the beatific vision as present in
Christ would mitigate all experience of authentic human
suffering. It is argued that the beatific vision in Christ's
soul would relegate his suffering as fictitious and his
redemption as ineffectual. The dilemma is expressed by
Galot in this way:

55. Galot, "Le Christ terrestre," 432, quoted in White, "Voluntary
Action of the Earthly Christ," 501. Hans Urs von Balthasar has argued similarly that this wide-ranging scope of knowledge in Jesus
stands in direct conflict with an authentic human life which is lived
with the possession of ignorance, see Balthasar, *You Crown the Year
with Your Goodness*, 318–19. O'Collins writes that the beatific vision
"would lift Christ's knowledge so clearly beyond the normal limits of
human knowledge as to cast serious doubts on the genuineness of his
humanity, at least in one essential aspect," see O'Collins, *Christology*,
256. Wolfhart Pannenberg exercises similar reservations, arguing
that "to attribute to the soul of Jesus a knowledge of all things past,
present, and future, and of everything that God knows from the very
beginning, in the sense of a supernatural vision, makes the danger
more than considerable that the genuine humanity of Jesus' experiential life would be lost," see Pannenberg, *Jesus—God and Man*, 329. For
a defense against Galot's claims of epistemological Monophysitism,
see White, "Voluntary Action of the Earthly Christ," 506–21.

> A Jesus whose soul would have been continually
> immersed in the beatific vision would have only
> assumed the exterior appearances of our human
> life. . . . His resemblance to us would only have
> been a facade. . . . What would become of the
> sufferings of the passion? . . . Not only does [the
> doctrine of the vision] put at risk the reality of
> the incarnation, but also that of the redemptive
> sacrifice. How can we attribute to a Savior who is
> filled with heavenly beatitude these words: 'My
> God, My God, why have you abandoned me?'
> . . . The cry of Jesus on the cross makes manifest
> the depths of a suffering that is incompatible
> with the beatitude of the vision.[56]

The final criticism reviewed is one that has been for-
mulated in recent years by Weinandy, who argues that the
attribution of the beatific vision to the Incarnate Christ
endangers certain orthodox christological truths made
about Jesus, specifically those declared at the Council of
Chalcedon in 451 AD which proclaimed Jesus to be one
person in two natures. According to Weinandy, the beatific
vision is traditionally understood as the immediate vision

56. Galot, "Le Christ terrestre," 434, quoted in White, "Voluntary
Action of the Earthly Christ," 502. O'Collins raises the same
objection, asking how it is that Christ can be said to have truly
suffered "if through his human mind he knew God immediately and
in a beatifying way," see O'Collins, *Christology*, 255. This apparent
contradiction was not left unrecognized by the medieval theologians.
For example, St. Thomas attempted to reconcile this tension by
advancing the idea that only the higher part of Christ's soul enjoyed
the blessed fruition during the passion, see Aquinas, *Summa
Theologica*, III, q. 46, a. 8. For a contemporary attempt at resolving
this tension, see White, "Jesus' Cry on the Cross and His Beatific
Vision," 555–82. For similar defenses that argue that the presence of
the beatific vision in the soul of Christ does not mitigate suffering,
but rather intensifies it, see Pitstick, *Light in Darkness*, 179–81; John
Paul II, *Novo Millennio Ineunte*, sec. 25–27.

of God by someone who is not God.[57] That is to say, in the beatific vision, the contemplator is not ontologically united to that which is contemplated.[58] The contemplated, rather, stands over and above the contemplator. This bears similarities to a Nestorian understanding of the ontology of Jesus, which views the incarnational act as the coming together of two different subjects, Jesus the man and Christ the Son, who are not ontologically united but instead stand over and above one another.[59] Consequently, the question of whether Jesus the man possessed the beatific vision could be answered positively in a Nestorian framework, since Jesus the man is not ontologically united to God and could, in fact, possess the vision. It is therefore argued by Weinandy that to attribute the beatific vision to the Incarnate Son would compromise his existence as a single hypostatic subject.[60]

57. Weinandy, "Jesus' Filial Vision of the Father," 190. Simon Francis Gaine, OP, has argued that Weinandy's definition of the beatific vision as "the immediate vision of God by someone who is not God" fails to take into account the Chalcedonian distinction between one person and two natures. Gaine maintains that Weinandy's definition should instead be nuanced as the immediate vision of God accessible to one who has a created mind, where the nature of the mind is distinguished from the level of the person, see Gaine, *Did the Saviour See the Father?*, 44.

58. Weinandy, "Jesus' Filial Vision of the Father," 190.

59. Weinandy, "Jesus' Filial Vision of the Father," 190.

60. Weinandy, "Jesus' Filial Vision of the Father," 190–92. This argument has been criticized by Neil Ormerod, who states that Weinandy's objection hinges on a "confrontationalist" understanding of knowledge where there is a primary split between the object and subject. Weinandy's argument immediately falls through, claims Ormerod, if one adopts an understanding of knowledge as assimilation between the knower and known, see Ormerod, "Doing the Will of the Father," 206, footnote 14, 209.

II. Karl Rahner

IN DECEMBER OF 1961, prominent theologian Karl Rahner presented a guest lecture before the Theological Faculty of Trier. The presentation was entitled "Dogmatic Reflections on the Knowledge and Self-Consciousness of Christ" and offered some reflections on the dogmatic declarations about Jesus and their implications for his knowledge and self-consciousness. The reflections of Rahner on this topic were significant for its challenge to the medieval synthesis of Jesus' human knowledge and, in particular, that of the beatific vision. In his presentation, Rahner offered a critique of the traditional notion of the beatific vision as ascribed to Jesus by Pius XII and essentially the whole theological tradition, claiming that such statements stand contrary to the authentic humanity and historical nature of Jesus, as witnessed to in the Scriptures and proclaimed at the Council of Chalcedon.[1] How can Jesus be described as one who increased in "wisdom" (Luke 2:52) if he possesses, at the moment of his conception, a knowledge of all things past, present, and to come? How could the Son plead ignorance in decisive matters of eschatology (Matt 24:36; Mark 13:32) if he possesses throughout his life a vision of

1. Rahner, "Dogmatic Reflections," 194–95.

the divine essence of God?[2] It seemed to Rahner that the long-established thesis of Jesus' beatific vision needed to be re-examined in order to become more compatible with the realities that are known about Christ, namely, the fact that the Son assumed a true human nature which subjected him to all the realities of the human condition save sin.

Preliminary Remarks and Methodology

Rahner's impact emerged as a result of his appreciation for human subjectivity in general and, in particular, the importance of *a priori* structures in the mind which function prior to the formation of themes and propositions.[3] In relation to this, Rahner ensured that he had first established several preliminary qualifications before proposing his answer on the issue of the Son's self-consciousness in relation to his own divine sonship. A hallmark in Rahner's work was the attention he gives to the intricacies involved in the functioning of human knowledge and consciousness, which he describes as "multi-dimensional structures."[4] Rahner thinks that this consideration is an important one and that it had not been taken into account previously when addressing the present question.[5] In the past, there had always been a recognition that there were different ways of attaining objective knowledge. One need only view the medieval threefold schema of Jesus' human knowledge which distinguished between beatific, infused, and acquired knowledge to recognize this. However, Rahner argues that these kinds of knowledge were always treated

---

2. Rahner, "Dogmatic Reflections," 195.

3. Moloney, "Mind of Christ in Transcendental Theology," 288.

4. Rahner, "Dogmatic Reflections," 199–200.

5. Rahner, "Dogmatic Reflections," 200.

as different ways of obtaining knowledge as opposed to being different ways of knowing one single reality.[6] This understanding had always carried with it a tacit presupposition that was traditionally assumed when dealing with the concept of man's knowing consciousness, that is, in association with the famous *tabula rasa* on which something is either written or not.[7] Rahner argued that this presupposition was an inadequate approach to the question of Jesus' knowledge since it failed to take into account the possibility of an object being known on one level and not on another at the same time.[8] With this in mind, Rahner made a distinction between the various kinds of consciousness, specifically distinguishing between reflexive consciousness and basic consciousness; the former understood as "clear, thematic and propositional" and the latter understood as "pre-conceptual, non-thematic and inarticulate."[9] This distinction is an important detail in Rahner's argument as he locates Jesus' vision of God within his basic consciousness, while the previous answers of exegetes could be described as placing it within his reflexive consciousness.[10]

Since the vision of God is placed in Christ's basic consciousness, it is important here to further explicate what is meant by basic consciousness. By this, Rahner is referring to an area of unthematic knowing that is the basic condition for the knowing of any kind of object. It is not constituted through the knowledge of an object but rather serves as the pre-condition for the knowing of the

6. Rahner, "Dogmatic Reflections," 200.

7. Rahner, "Dogmatic Reflections," 200.

8. Rahner, "Dogmatic Reflections," 199. Moloney claims that this understanding was consistent with the insights of modern empirical psychology, see Moloney, *Knowledge of Christ,* 83.

9. Moloney, *Knowledge of Christ,* 83.

10. Moloney, *Knowledge of Christ,* 84.

conscious subject.[11] It is not often thought about and is commonly taken for granted. It is possible to reflect on it and express that which is perceived in basic consciousness, however, even this expression is limited and, to some extent, historically-conditioned.[12] The failure to articulate this basic awareness through thematic words and concepts does not thereby render the perceptions present in the basic consciousness as fictitious or unreal. Rather, it reveals the innermost experience of the conscious subject, an experience which is immediate and self-present without any need for reflection. This is an important consideration as the placement of Jesus' vision of God in the depths of his basic consciousness, rather than in his reflexive consciousness, means that God is present in the basic condition of Jesus, both immediately and to some extent, inexpressibly. Furthermore, this distinction between reflexive and basic consciousness makes room for the idea that Jesus' knowledge was subject to both development and ignorance over the course of his life, as seemingly portrayed in the Gospel accounts.[13]

Another important consideration in the work of Rahner is his reinterpretation of the nature of Jesus' vision. Rather than qualifying the vision as "beatific," Rahner thought that it was more cautious and precise to

11. Moloney, "Mind of Christ in Transcendental Theology," 289.

12. Rahner, "Dogmatic Reflections," 201. This view will remain important for our discussion on the kind of development that Rahner allows for in Jesus' vision.

13. With this framework in mind, Jesus' vision of God and, by consequence, his awareness of his divine identity could be secured by being placed within Christ's basic consciousness, while any notion of ignorance or development in the knowledge of the Son could be satisfied by locating it in his reflexive consciousness, see Moloney, "Mind of Christ in Transcendental Theology," 289.

speak of the vision as "immediate."[14] He argues that it is a misconception to identify the immediacy and nearness of God, that is, the direct presence of God to one's soul as always necessarily constituting a beatifying effect.[15] Additionally, Rahner thought that his conception of the *visio immediata* was more compatible with the Gospel accounts as it attributes to Christ the direct presence of God while at the same time avoids having to ascribe to Christ perfect beatific fruition throughout his life. For example, was it possible to maintain that Jesus enjoyed perfect and constant joy in the beatific vision while simultaneously crying out on the cross, "My God, my God, why hast thou forsaken me?" (Matt 27:46). It seemed to Rahner that the only way to side-step this apparent tension, without adding "an artificial layer-psychology," was to reconceive the manner of Jesus' vision as "immediate" rather than "beatific."[16]

In regard to his methodology, Rahner does not aim to provide a comprehensive work of biblical exegesis on the subject-matter but he intends that his reflections be taken as purely dogmatic considerations. The aim of his work is to provide a "conceivable theological conception" that does not stand in contradiction with the previous declarations of the Church's magisterium on the issue.[17] According to Rahner, theologians are bound to maintain the notion of Jesus possessing a vision of God in his human soul. However, the manner in which this vision is to be conceived is open to interpretation.[18] The premise

14. Rahner, "Current Problems," 170, footnote 2.
15. Rahner, "Dogmatic Reflections," 203.
16. Rahner, "Dogmatic Reflections," 203.
17. Rahner, "Dogmatic Reflections," 199.
18. Rahner, "Dogmatic Reflections," 213.

by which Rahner begins his work is with the binding theological truths declared about Christ—in particular, the certain christological truths that were expressed at the Council of Chalcedon. It is from here that Rahner thinks the issue of Jesus' self-consciousness and human knowledge can be resolved, stating that his theory "seems to make sense because it seems to prove itself to be deductible from dogmatic presuppositions which are certain."[19] The dogmatic presupposition that Rahner refers to here is the reality of the "Hypostatic Union of the Logos with a human nature in Jesus Christ" which serves as the basis for any dogmatic statements concerning the self-consciousness and human knowledge of Jesus.[20] Hence, in the Rahnerian framework, the way in which to approach this question is through considering the ontological constitution of the person of Christ, namely, the reality of the hypostatic union and the deducible implications that follow from it. Rahner also admits that there exists a certain tension between the dogmatic theologian and the exegete and that the two, at least up until now, have consciously avoided treading on the territory of the other.[21] With this insight in mind, Rahner's goal was to present a theory that was compatible with the accounts of Scripture. As said, he did not provide a comprehensive work of exegesis but intended to "offer the exegete a dogmatic conception of Christ's self-consciousness and knowledge which will perhaps make it easier than it has been in the face of previous conceptions for him to admit that this conception is compatible with his own historical findings. We say: that it is 'compatible'.

---

19. Rahner, "Dogmatic Reflections," 199.
20. Rahner, "Dogmatic Reflections," 198–99.
21. Rahner, "Dogmatic Reflections," 195.

For this is all that is required."[22] In retrospect, the influence of Rahner on this issue was largely significant, to the extent that his reflection helped to alleviate the deadlock that existed between dogmatic theology and exegesis, as well as set new foundations for all subsequent reflection concerning the present question.[23]

Thomistic Axioms and Christ's Immediate Vision

With these preliminary qualifications in mind, we come to the main body of Rahner's argument. Here he begins with the axiom of the Thomistic metaphysics of knowledge which claims that being and self-awareness are held together in a primeval union.[24] In this understanding, the self-consciousness of an existent is constituted upon the degree "in which it has or is being."[25] Rahner states that "[t]he higher an entity . . . in its grade of being, compactness of being, 'actuality', the more intelligible it is and present to itself."[26] Rahner also maintains this position elsewhere, contending that being and consciousness are in fact the same thing and that an entity is "present to itself" in accordance with its degree of act.[27] It is sometimes being argued that Rahner's interpretation of

22. Rahner, "Dogmatic Reflections," 198. Exegetes have often acknowledged their appreciation for the work of Rahner in relation to the present question, see Moloney, "Mind of Christ in Transcendental Theology," 288.

23. Moloney, *Knowledge of Christ,* 88.

24. Moloney, "Mind of Christ in Transcendental Theology," 289.

25. Rahner, "Dogmatic Reflections," 205.

26. Rahner, "Current Problems," 169.

27. Rahner, *Foundations of Christian Faith,* 303.

this axiom bears more resemblance with German idealism than that of classical Thomism.[28] Nevertheless, Rahner's presupposition of this axiom is a vital constituent for the remainder of his answer to the current question. With this axiomatic principle in mind, Rahner turns his sight to the ontological constitution of Christ, which, in accordance with the declarations of Chalcedon, consists of two natures: divine and human. The reality of the hypostatic union, which "implies the self-communication of the absolute Being of God—such as it subsists in the Logos— to the human nature of Christ which thereby becomes a nature hypostatically supported by the Logos" is the ontologically highest actualization of a creature apart from God's being.[29] Furthermore, according to the presupposed axiom, that which is ontologically highest must, by

28. Moloney, *Knowledge of Christ*, 103, footnote 14. Benedict Ashley, OP, has stated that most Thomists "do not accept this interpretation of Aquinas, since it colors his thought with the philosophy of Kant, who claimed for us an *a priori* element in human knowledge independent of the senses," see Ashley, "Extent of Jesus' Human Knowledge," 249.

29 Rahner, "Dogmatic Reflections," 205. It seems as though Rahner derived this principle from Maurice de la Taille's theory on created actuation by uncreated act. Concerning the hypostatic union, de la Taille states that "[b]eyond this unity of Person in which the hypostatic union terminates, nothing further is possible: and this is why the grace of union is, even as regards the divine omnipotence itself, the pinnacle of likeness to God. It substantially conforms the human nature to the substance of the Word. . . . [T]his union which, being substantial, occupies the highest possible summit among all the communications of the pure Act to a created potency," see de la Taille, "Created Actuation by Uncreated Act," 41. For more information on de la Taille's theory, see Donnelly, "The Theory of R. P. Maurice De La Taille, S.J.," 510–26. It is perhaps worth noting some of the criticisms made by Lonergan concerning de la Taille's famous theorem in Lonergan, *Ontological and Psychological Constitution of Christ*, 57–59; Lonergan, *The Incarnate Word*, 439.

necessity, be conscious of itself.[30] If an existent that is ontologically lower is aware of its own self, then this must also be the case for that which is ontologically higher, that is, the created human nature as it subsists in the Logos.[31] Therefore, Jesus must necessarily be conscious of himself by virtue of his ontological constitution and in accordance with this axiomatic principle concerning being and self-consciousness. Moreover, it is through the existence of the hypostatic union that Jesus possesses the *visio immediata,* which Rahner describes as the "conscious being-with-the-Logos of Christ's soul."[32] This means that the direct vision of God that the human soul of Jesus possesses is, in fact, the vision of the Logos himself.[33] Rahner describes it in this way:

> For this direct presence to God is the plain, simple self-awareness—the necessary self-realisation—of the substantial union with the person of the Logos himself . . . this and nothing more. This means, however, that this really existing direct vision of God is nothing other than the original unobjectified consciousness of divine sonship, which is present by the mere fact that there *is* a Hypostatic Union.[34]

30. Rahner, "Dogmatic Reflections," 206.

31. Rahner, "Dogmatic Reflections," 206.

32. Rahner, "Current Problems," 170. Rahner claims that this vision is not an extrinsic addition to the hypostatic union, but rather is an "intrinsic and inalienable element of this Union," see Rahner, "Dogmatic Reflections," 215.

33. Moloney, "Mind of Christ in Transcendental Theology," 296.

34. Rahner, "Dogmatic Reflections," 208 (emphasis original). This idea is expressed elsewhere by Rahner when he states that "our Lord's self-consciousness, which we have here inferred metaphysically from the *unio hypostatica,* is—in its source and primarily at least—a given quantity which must be thought of as being situated in that

Although Rahner uses the term "vision" more or less throughout his work, he makes note of the complications associated with its use. For example, when one speaks of the "vision" that Jesus possessed, the image of "vision" that immediately makes itself present in the mind is one of an object (the Word) being looked at by the observer (Christ) who stands opposite to it.[35] Rahner wants to avoid this image of "vision" at all costs and so claims that it is more appropriate in this case to refer to the "direct presence to God" in the human soul of Jesus.[36] In substantiating how best to understand this direct presence, Rahner compares it to the "intellectually subjective basic condition of human spirituality in general."[37] This means that the direct presence of the Logos to the human soul of Jesus functions in the same way as the basic condition of the spiritual man, who, without thought or reflection, is conscious of his own spiritual nature, transcendence, and freedom.[38] This basic condition is immediately present to the spiritual subject without the need for ever having to reflect on or

---

substantial depth of Christ's created mind which becomes aware of itself in the act of knowledge, *pointing ontically beyond itself to that with which it is united, the Logos*" (emphasis added), see Rahner, "Current Problems," 171.

35. Rahner, "Dogmatic Reflections," 207.

36. Rahner states that "this direct presence is the same kind of presence as is meant by the '*visio immediata*', except that it excludes the element of 'standing opposite' an object, an element which is usually associated with it as soon as one forms an image of 'vision'; we can quite rightly speak of a vision even in this case, as long as we exclude from our notion of vision this particular element of an objective, intentional counter-pole," see Rahner, "Dogmatic Reflections," 209.

37. Rahner, "Dogmatic Reflections," 208.

38. Rahner, "Dogmatic Reflections," 208.

form propositions about what these realities in fact are.[39] Although one can reflect on this all-pervading basic condition, it certainly cannot be comprehended to its full extent. Knowledge attained through reflection remains as mere information about the basic condition and is not the basic condition itself.[40] The ineffable nature of this basic condition is best explained by Rahner in the following passage:

> [I]t is not necessary that the reflection on this basic condition should succeed; it may perhaps even be impossible, and its never quite success-ful exercise may depend on the external, histori-cally contingent data of external experience, on the conceptual material offered from elsewhere and on its historical character.[41]

Two main points may be extracted here for our investigation. These are that the basic condition of the spiritual man cannot be expressed to its full extent and that if ever one attempted to explain this basic condition, the resultant explanation would be subject to and dependent upon the historical conditioning of the subject. With this consideration in mind, the basic condition of man becomes the hermeneutical key by which to imagine how the direct presence of the Logos to the human soul of Jesus operates, as well as the way in which this presence

39. Rahner, "Dogmatic Reflections," 208.

40. Rahner articulates this point in this way: "The conceptually reflex knowledge of it, even when it is present, is never this condition itself but is always supported by it in its turn and for this reason alone never gets an adequate grasp of this basic condition," see Rahner, "Dogmatic Reflections," 201. This argument seems especially coherent given the fact that any conceptualization about the basic condition both presupposes and requires its existence.

41. Rahner, "Dogmatic Reflections," 201.

is subject to development within the spiritual history of Jesus.[42] For example, Rahner explains that although the basic condition of man as a spiritual being is known in an immediate and unreflective way, man must nevertheless still come to learn over time how best to *express* these realities as they are present in his basic condition.[43] Man must "come to himself" so as to reflectively process and articulate in a systematic and objectified way that which has always been present in the depths of his basic condition.[44] This understanding is applied to the self-consciousness of Jesus whereby the Son, although always having been conscious of his divine sonship, must learn within his historical environment how best to communicate this awareness as present to him in his basic condition.[45] Thus, the development that takes place in Jesus is not an increase in the "immediacy" of the direct presence to the soul of Christ but rather concerns how this presence is expressed by Jesus in human words and concepts.[46] As previously mentioned, the articulation of the spiritual man's basic condition is subject to influence by one's own external historical surroundings. One cannot attempt to interpret

42. Rahner's assumption here is that this direct presence to God in the basic condition of Jesus demands "a genuinely human spiritual history and development of the man Jesus," see Rahner, "Dogmatic Reflections," 210.

43. Rahner, "Dogmatic Reflections," 210–11.

44. Rahner, "Dogmatic Reflections," 211.

45. Rahner, "Dogmatic Reflections," 211.

46. Of this, Rahner states that "this development does not refer to the establishment of the basic state of direct presence to God but to the objective, humanly and conceptually expressed articulation and objectification of this basic state. . . . Such a development, far from denying the fact of his absolute, conscious and direct presence to the Logos, is based on this fact and interprets and objectifies it," see Rahner, "Dogmatic Reflections," 211.

themselves without taking into account the religious and cultural age that they themselves were immersed in. In this way, Rahner thinks that it is legitimate to assume that Jesus used his religious environment so as to better grapple with and explain to others the reality of his divine sonship.[47] He states:

> In principle, at least, such a history of his self-declaration has in no way to be interpreted merely as a history of his pedagogical accommodation, but can quite legitimately be seen also as the history of his own personal *self-*interpretation of himself to himself. For this does not mean that Jesus 'discovered something' which he did not know in any way up until then, but it means rather that he grasped more and more what he already always is and basically also already knows.[48]

47. Rahner, "Dogmatic Reflections," 212. Regarding this view, Moloney explains: "In this process Jesus would be assisted by his growing knowledge of his environment, and inevitably his eventual articulation of his divine identity would be expressed in terms of his own culture and history," see Moloney, *Knowledge of Christ*, 87. White seems to affirm this point, arguing that "the Son of God would deliberate and think like any other historical human being, employing terms and concepts of his epoch," see White, "Dyotheletism and the Instrumental Human Consciousness of Jesus," 419. Adding to this, the *Catechism of the Catholic Church* acknowledges this idea that the human knowledge of Jesus "was exercised in the historical conditions of his existence in space and time" and that Jesus "would even have to inquire for himself about what one in the human condition can learn only from experience," see *Catechism of the Catholic Church*, 472.

48. Rahner, "Dogmatic Reflections," 212 (emphasis original).

Secondary Objects of Knowledge

Earlier in his reflections, Rahner offered a critique of the Greek ideal of man which understands nescience as an attribute that is devoid of any positive function. Historically speaking, it had mostly been viewed as the hill by which man must climb so as to progress towards perfection. With this understanding in mind, Rahner, while offering an account that was by no means exhaustive, argued that nescience does, in fact, possess a positive use insofar as it is a necessary condition for the freedom of individual acts. He states that "freedom in the open field of decisions is better than if this room for freedom were filled with knowledge of such a nature as to suffocate this freedom."[49] In attempting to explicate a positive function of nescience, Rahner wanted to reconcile the tension that had existed for centuries between the perfection of Jesus and his supposed ignorance, as well as having to avoid asserting that Jesus possessed some kind of quasi-omniscience during his life on earth. He explains that there are no magisterial pronouncements that bind theologians to hold to the idea that Jesus had a "permanent, reflex and fully-formed propositional knowledge of everything after the manner of an encyclopedia or of a huge, actually completed world-history."[50] He instead concedes that the scope of the objects contained in Jesus' vision pertains only to the "implicit knowledge of everything connected with the mission and soteriological task of Our Lord."[51]

49. Rahner, "Dogmatic Reflections," 214. Rahner's insistence on ignorance as a necessary condition for freedom runs contrary to the thought of St. Thomas, see Aquinas, *Summa Theologica,* III, q. 18, a. 4, ad. 1.

50. Rahner, "Dogmatic Reflections," 214.

51. Rahner, "Dogmatic Reflections," 213.

Adding to this, Rahner chose to locate these secondary objects, including Jesus' knowledge of "the last things," in the same realm as the direct presence, that is, in the basic consciousness of Christ.[52] It seems, however, that Rahner did not directly treat the question of Jesus' knowledge as it relates to the particular individuals for whom he gave his life. In spite of this, it appears that Rahner wished to attribute to Jesus an immediate and comprehensive knowledge of all things as they related to his life and mission and yet, as was the case with the "direct presence," Christ's expression of this awareness was subject to both limitations and developments, as well as bore the mark of historical conditioning.[53]

Criticisms

Rahner's theory served as a breakthrough away from the traditional thesis on the threefold human knowledge of Jesus. It not only adequately preserved the understanding that Jesus was certainly aware of himself as God, but was also able to account for development in the self-consciousness of the Son. His thesis also competently coincided with the insights of empirical psychology and set new paths for scholars who wished to undertake this topic as an area of future research. It has been said that it feels as though the only positions available on the whole question of Christ's self-consciousness lay between the traditional scholastic position and the Rahnerian alternative.[54] Although Rahner's theory was commendable in a variety of ways, it was still not without its problems.

52. Rahner, "Dogmatic Reflections," 215.
53. Rahner, "Dogmatic Reflections," 215.
54. Moloney, *Knowledge of Christ*, 300.

Criticism could be made about the way Rahner interpreted the vision of Jesus, choosing to qualify it as "the direct and personal presence of the Logos to the human soul of Jesus."[55] This formulation seems problematic in light of the scriptural evidence which portrays the life and work of Christ as one that is heavily centered on the Father. Without attempting to enter into debate about certain considerations that can be made regarding redaction criticism and the Gospels, a brief overview will nonetheless be attempted to be highlighted here. Throughout the Gospels, Jesus declares a number of things about himself which always incorporate in some way his relation to the Father. He declares that he is one with the Father (John 10:30; 14:11; 17:21), receives life from the Father (John 6:57; 8:42), has been sent from the Father and is returning to the Father (John 16:28; 20:17; 20:21), claims to be the only one who has known and has seen the Father (Matt 11:27; Luke 10:22; John 1:18; 6:46; 17:25), that he is loved by the Father (John 3:35; 5:20; 10:17), instructs his disciples to pray to the Father (Matt 6:9; Luke 11:2), remains obedient to the Father's will (Mark 14:36; Matt 26:39; Luke 22:42; John 14:31), and announces that he is the only way to the Father (John 14:6). This list, while not being exhaustive, supports the idea that the focal point of Jesus' life and mission stood in relation to the Father and not just himself. Jesus comes as a herald of the Father to proclaim the Father's love to the world. It would then seem an appropriate assertion to describe the New Testament accounts of Jesus' life and mission as heavily patricentric, that is, as centered on his relationship with his Father. With these considerations in mind, Rahner's conception of the vision as the "human soul of Jesus knowing the Logos" seems to run contrary to

55. Rahner, "Dogmatic Reflections," 210.

the evidence contained in the texts of the New Testament. This is perhaps the largest criticism that one could posit about Rahner's theory, namely, that the Son becomes self-conscious in relation to his own divinity rather than in relation to the Father.

This very point has been criticized by a number of different authors, even those who are sympathetic to the work of Rahner.[56] For example, Walter Kasper identified Rahner's treatment of the self-consciousness of Jesus as predicated on the hypostatic union as incompatible with the New Testament data which describes the mind of Christ as centered on the Father, not the Logos.[57] It has also been argued that Rahner's understanding of the vision treats the human soul of Jesus and the Logos as two distinct subjects, thus "raising the spectre of a Nestorian duality of subjects."[58] Such criticism has been advanced by Weinandy, who once remarked that Rahner's thesis bore the taste of Nestorianism. According to Weinandy, Rahner treats the divinity as an object to be known by the Son as opposed to the Son becoming subjectively self-conscious of his own divinity.[59] Weinandy argued that this posited two existing "I's" in Rahner's thesis, that is, the "I" of the knower, Jesus, and the "I" of the divinity, namely, the Logos, who stands ontologically distinct as the object to be known.[60] It would seem that Rahner in his later works did

56. Moloney, "Mind of Christ in Transcendental Theology," 296.

57. Kasper, *Jesus the Christ*, 271, footnote 60. For another critic on the same point, see Riedlinger, *Geschichtlichkeit und Vollendung*, 152–53, quoted in Moloney, *Knowledge of Christ*, 103, footnote 19. One could also note Balthasar's affirmation of Riedlinger's criticism in Balthasar, *Dramatis Personae: Persons in Christ*, 172–73.

58. Moloney, *Knowledge of Christ*, 128.

59. Weinandy, "Human 'I' of Jesus," 266–67, footnote 4.

60. Weinandy, "Human 'I' of Jesus," 266–67, footnote 4.

not turn a blind eye to these kinds of criticisms, choosing instead to describe the "vision" as merely the human soul of Jesus centered on "God," rather than the Word.[61]

Another possible criticism concerns the Rahnerian treatment of the secondary objects of the vision. As noted earlier, Rahner places these secondary objects in Christ's basic consciousness while describing the measure of this scope as extending only to that which pertains to Jesus' life and mission. This idea has been criticized by Helmut Riedlinger, who states that a conception such as this opens the back door for a "relative omniscience" in Christ.[62] This is because Rahner claims that Jesus, in his basic condition, absolutely knows "the last things" in the same way that he absolutely knows himself to be the Son of God. However, in the objective translation of his basic condition, he knows them insofar as this condition can be given "a historically conditioned and *a-posteriori* expression."[63]

A final criticism that could be suggested is Rahner's retention of traditional terminology while, at the same time, radically redefining these terms to mean something wholly distinct from their original meaning.[64] For example,

61. Rahner states: "And I must believe that Jesus' human soul, as a human soul, contemplates in adoration from an infinite distance of creatureliness what is for it, too, the enduring incomprehensibility of God," see Rahner, "Christology Today," 222–23. This can be compared to his earlier comments in *Theological Investigations* vol. 1, where he writes that the human nature of the Logos "possesses a genuine, spontaneous, free, spiritual, active centre, a human selfconsciousness, which as creaturely faces the eternal Word in a genuinely human attitude of adoration, obedience, a most radical sense of creaturehood," see Rahner, "Current Problems," 158.

62. Riedlinger, *Geschichtlichkeit und Vollendung*, 152–53, quoted in Moloney, *Knowledge of Christ*, 103, footnote 23.

63. Rahner, "Dogmatic Reflections," 215.

64. John Ashton, SJ, remarked that as a theologian, Rahner possessed "an almost obsessive determination to retain traditional

II. KARL RAHNER

Rahner states that in order to do justice to the previous magisterial declarations on the issue, theologians must hold fast to the idea that the human soul of Jesus possessed a "vision" of God during his earthly life.[65] Throughout his reflection, however, Rahner shifts between the notions of vision and consciousness, qualifying "vision" as the "original, unobjectified consciousness of divine sonship" present through the hypostatic union.[66] Such a dramatic qualification of the term "vision" seems to provide justification for any contemporary theologian who wishes to do away with the traditional notions of "beatific" and "vision" in relation to the present question.[67] John Ashton, SJ, notes that "[n]othing in his [Rahner's] explanation of what the 'immediate vision' consists in justifies the use of a word whose central core of meaning is evacuated by his own qualifications."[68] Therefore, at first instance, there appears to be uniformity between Rahner's thesis and the previous tradition regarding Jesus' vision. However, upon further investigation, one soon comes to the realization that what Rahner means by "immediate vision" stands largely distinct from what has been understood for centuries about the vision that Jesus possessed, insofar as Rahner chooses to qualify the "beatific vision" as the "non-beatific, immediate, direct presence of the Word to the human soul of Jesus."

---

terminology even when he has re-interpreted the tradition itself beyond all recognition," see Ashton, "Consciousness of Christ I," 68, footnote 1.

65. Rahner, "Dogmatic Reflections," 215.

66. Rahner, "Dogmatic Reflections," 208.

67. Ashton, "Consciousness of Christ I," 68.

68. Ashton, "Consciousness of Christ I," 68.

III. Thomas Weinandy

IN RELATIVELY RECENT YEARS, Thomas Weinandy has written ample material on the present question of Christ's self-consciousness and his human knowledge. Writing during the modern christological current has allowed Weinandy to provide both useful insights as well as impactful criticisms on the previous formulations regarding Jesus' self-consciousness. This can be seen with respect to the preceding authors, whose theses, according to Weinandy, result in a conception of Christ that is Nestorian. In the case of the beatific vision, it is argued by Weinandy that this vision implies an ontological division between Jesus and God since the one who receives the beatific vision stands ontologically distinct from the object of the vision, namely, God. Concerning the Rahnerian treatment of Jesus' vision, Weinandy holds that Rahner's notion of the *visio immediata* where the soul of Jesus contemplates the Logos implies an ontological separation of "I's," that is, one for the knower, i.e., Jesus, and one for the known, i.e., the Logos. With these concerns in mind, Weinandy, with deep fidelity to the Cyrillian tradition, aims to create a conception of the vision of Jesus that both informs the Incarnate Son of his divine identity while, at the same time, avoids positing any ontological dualism in the Son of God made man. In order to accomplish this, the object that is present in Jesus' vision must not be an object that is ontologically distinct from the Son.[1] This will ensure that there is no subordination of the Son to the Father and will thereby uphold Jesus' identity as true God. It is also imperative for Weinandy that the divinity is not treated as an object which Jesus comes to discover. This would be to treat the divinity as a transcendent object ontologically separate from the one subject, Jesus.[2] In order to avoid such problems, Weinandy argues that the Son, rather than coming to know or discover his divine identity as an object ontologically distinct from himself, must instead become subjectively self-conscious of his identity as the Son. This means that the one who experiences the vision cannot be a subject apart from the Son, nor can the object of the vision be an object that is ontologically distinct from the Son.[3] It is these theological considerations that shape Weinandy's understanding of the nature of Jesus' vision.

Preliminary Remarks and Methodology

Rather than beginning with the fact of the hypostatic union or from Thomistic axioms of knowledge as Maritain and Rahner would, Weinandy instead begins with the whole act of the Incarnation. The entire question of Jesus' self-awareness is, for Weinandy, predicated on the reality of and on the principles embodied in the Incarnation of the Logos. Thus, in order to elucidate how Weinandy conceives of the vision of Jesus, it is first necessary to delineate how Weinandy understands the incarnational "becoming,"

1. Weinandy, "Jesus' Filial Vision of the Father," 192.
2. Weinandy, "Human 'I' of Jesus," 266–67, footnote 4.
3. Weinandy, "Jesus' Filial Vision of the Father," 192.

that is, what does it mean to say that the Son of God became man?

In seeking continuity with the theology of Cyril of Alexandria and the Council of Chalcedon, Weinandy argues that the incarnational "becoming" has to be read in personal/existential terms.[4] It is not a compositional union of two incompatible natures as some contemporary christologists suggest, especially those who endorse a kenotic Christology. Weinandy claims that an erroneous approach to the Incarnation rests on this foundation when the Incarnation is interpreted first through the two natures and only then their union.[5] This starting point inevitably leads to an undermining of either the divine or human nature of Jesus.[6] In order to rightly interpret the incarnational "becoming," three interrelated truths must be maintained, which are as follows: It is truly the Son of God who is man; it is truly man that the Son of God is; the Son of God truly is man.[7] These three truths form the foundation of Weinandy's personal/existential reading of the Incarnation. That is, in regard to the person of the Incarnation, it is truly the

4. Weinandy, *Does God Change?*, 54.

5. It is this approach that led to Nestorius's rejection of Christ as a single ontological subject. Weinandy states: "The failure of Nestorius to account for a substantial union in Christ and thus a true Incarnation lay in the fact that he began with the natures distinct and individual, and then tried to put them together," see Weinandy, *Does God Change?*, 46–47.

6. Weinandy writes: "They [the kenotic christologists] envisage the act of incarnating as the bringing together and uniting of two contrary and incompatible natures or essences (divine and human) containing within themselves contradictory attributes (for example, omniscience and limited knowledge; omnipotence and limited power). Such an essentialist understanding always leads, by necessity, to the Nestorian conundrum," see Weinandy, *In the Likeness of Sinful Flesh,* 10–11.

7. Weinandy, "Jesus' Filial Vision of the Father," 192.

Son of God who is Incarnate. In terms of his existence, it is truly man that the Son of God is. The person or "who" of the Incarnation is the Son of God, while the manner of his existence or his "how" is as man.[8] Thus, the incarnational becoming for Weinandy cannot be read in terms of two incompatible natures, divine and human, coming together to form the man, Jesus. It has to be read, Weinandy insists, through a personal/existential lens, whereby the Son of God comes to exist in a new manner or mode, namely, as man.[9]

To substantiate the degree to which Weinandy is insistent that the Incarnation must be viewed in this personal/existential manner, it is important to turn to Weinandy's conception of the nature of Jesus' "I." In aiming to preserve the incarnational truths communicated by Cyril, Weinandy argues that Jesus, throughout his human life, possessed an "I" that was well and truly human.[10] However, as Weinandy admits, this assertion has a "Nestorian ring" to it.[11] The reason for this is that the nature of the "I" is commonly perceived, especially among the scholastic philosophers, to correspond with the nature of the person.[12] Therefore, if

8. Weinandy, *Does God Change?*, 54.

9. Weinandy states that "classical Christology, as the Council of Chalcedon defined it and such theologians as St. Cyril of Alexandria and St. Thomas Aquinas interpreted it, is not essentialistic, but personal/existential. The Incarnation is not the fusing together of two incompatible natures (divine and human), but the person of the Son coming to exist as man or coming to be man," see Weinandy, *In the Likeness of Sinful Flesh*, 11.

10. Weinandy, *In the Likeness of Sinful Flesh*, 12–13.

11. Weinandy, "Human 'I' of Jesus," 259.

12. Lonergan, *Ontological and Psychological Constitution of Christ*, 171. On this point, Galot concurs: "To affirm that Christ has a human 'I' therefore entails a certain danger of ambiguity, for it might seem to imply that there is a human person in him," see Galot, *Who is Christ?*, 330.

it were true that Jesus possessed an "I" that was human, the resultant conclusion would be that this human "I" corresponded to the existence of a human person. This is why theologians in the past, who held valid the Chalcedonian dogma of Jesus as a single divine person, were quite hesitant to attribute to Christ a human "I," and why other theologians who argued for a human "I" in Christ did so from a Nestorian perspective.[13] Understanding these concerns, Weinandy believes that it is still appropriate to attribute to Christ an "I" that is distinctly human and that such an attribution to the Incarnate Son renders no harm to his existence as a single divine subject.[14] This is because the "I" that Jesus possesses does not correspond to a human person, Weinandy claims, but rather relates to the manner of the Son's existence.[15] He argues that in truly becoming man, the Son possessed a thoroughly human manner of relating to others.[16] He did not communicate with others through his divine transcendence, which would be the case if the Son had never become Incarnate.[17] Rather, the Son, in truly becoming man, came to live, act, and express himself in a manner that was authentically human.[18] In this way, the Son of God made man was able

13. Weinandy, "Human 'I' of Jesus," 266–67, footnote 4.

14. Weinandy, "Human 'I' of Jesus," 263.

15. Weinandy, "Human 'I' of Jesus," 263.

16. Weinandy, *In the Likeness of Sinful Flesh*, 12.

17. Weinandy, "Human 'I' of Jesus," 264.

18. Weinandy states: "As incarnate, the Son possessed (and possesses) a human personality, a thoroughly human manner of relating. Jesus possessed not only a human body, mind, and will, but also a human centre of self-consciousness, a human self-identity. He thought and spoke with the integrity of a thoroughly human 'I'. He was self-conscious, composed his thoughts, and spoke in an entirely human manner, with the human 'I' of a man," see Weinandy, *In the Likeness of Sinful Flesh*, 12.

to establish horizontal relationships with other humans, communicating with them through their very own mode of human expression.[19] This was made possible through the Son's human psychological center of self-expression, or through his human "I" for short.[20] Weinandy explains:

> To profess that the Son of God, the one person, exists as man, confirms that the Son now lives and functions under the conditions of a human being, as a man. Thus the divine Son, as incarnate, not only lives and acts within the confines of a human will and human intellect, but he also is conscious and knows himself within the confines of a human self-consciousness.[21]

19. Weinandy writes: "Between the incarnate Son of God and other human beings, there is an encounter of equal 'I's,'" see Weinandy, "Human 'I' of Jesus," 264. Galot agrees that the Son of God made man possessed a human manner of relating with his followers: "In becoming man, the relational being of the Son inaugurated horizontal relationships with men. His contacts were no longer directed solely downward from above. They were henceforth to be made on a level of equality with human nature. Through this human nature, a divine relational being entered into human interpersonal relations," see Galot, *Who is Christ?*, 307.

20. Galot, despite holding to the idea that Jesus possessed an "I" that was divine, nevertheless states that this divine "I" had a human mode of expression. He writes: "Obviously, we are not speaking of a divine 'I' that manifests itself as such in its pure state, but of a divine 'I' in a human context, of an 'I' that asserts itself within a human consciousness and in human language. It is the divine 'I' of a man who is living a genuinely human life," see Galot, *Who is Christ?*, 321–22.

21. Weinandy, "Human 'I' of Jesus," 263–64. Galot again shares a similar viewpoint, stating: "A normal consequence of the Incarnation is that the Son of God became the subject of human psychological activity. In becoming man and assuming a human nature, he exercised the activity proper to this nature," see Galot, *Who is Christ?*, 337. Lonergan concurs with this assessment, stating that the Son as man must become conscious in a manner that is properly human. He

III. THOMAS WEINANDY

For Weinandy, the human "I" corresponds to the manner or mode of the Incarnate Son's existence, where he lives, speaks, and acts as man. It was as man, through his human mind and self-consciousness, that Jesus spoke, built relationships with, and communicated to others divine truths.[22] However, this "I" does not correspond to a human person, but rather signifies the mode of existence of the one divine subject. It is the human "I" of a divine "who," and this "I" must necessarily be human since it is truly man that the Son of God became.[23] Hence, it can be said that the human "I" gives expression to that with which it is ontologically united, the divine Son.[24] This notion of the human "I" of Jesus is an important underlying premise for establishing the nature of the Incarnate Son's vision.[25]

Jesus' Filial Vision of the Father

In order to maintain the "who" of the Incarnation as the pre-existent Logos, and not some other subject that has come into being at the time of the Incarnation, two things are imperative to note. The first is that the vision that is possessed by Christ cannot be a vision of an ontological reality that exists apart from himself, and the second is

states that "through a consciousness that is truly and properly human, a divine person is conscious of a divine person," see Lonergan, *Ontological and Psychological Constitution of Christ*, 211.

22. Weinandy, "Human 'I' of Jesus," 265.

23. Weinandy, "Jesus' Filial Vision of the Father," 195.

24. Weinandy, "Human 'I' of Jesus," 264.

25. It seems that Weinandy here stands guilty of the same criticism that has been made of Rahner's work, namely, that although he has retained traditional terminology throughout his work, i.e., the "I" of Jesus, he has reinterpreted the nature of this term so as to denote something wholly distinct from its classical meaning.

that the vision cannot be experienced by anyone other than the divine Son himself. To uphold the "how" of Jesus' existence, namely, that he lives, acts, and expresses himself in an authentically human manner within the parameters of his human "I," the Son must become *humanly* aware of his identity as the Son. As Thomas Joseph White, OP, describes, if Jesus is to personally stand in relation to God intellectually, then the vision that Jesus experiences must be a human vision.[26] It is a human vision possessed by the Son which allows him to actively cognize, in a human manner, his identity as the Son of the Father. This vision is referred to by Weinandy as the Son's "human filial vision of the Father."[27] He states:

> [W]hile the subject of any such vision of the Father must be the Son and not another 'who' apart from the Son, it is *as man*, since this is the manner of the Son's *incarnate existence,* that the Son possesses such a vision, for it is as man that the Son becomes humanly conscious of himself as Son through his human vision of the Father.[28]

The Son's filial vision is a personal vision where the Son comes to see the Father as his own Father and, in seeing the Father, comes to see himself as the Son of

26. White, "Voluntary Action of the Earthly Christ," 504.

27. This vision is also referred to as the Son's "hypostatic vision of the Father" in Weinandy's earlier works on the subject, see Weinandy, "Jesus' Filial Vision of the Father," 193. However, in his later works, Weinandy more commonly refers to this vision as the Son's "filial vision of the Father." Although the nature of these visions is not opposed, I will refer to Weinandy's conception of Jesus' vision only as his "filial vision of the Father" as opposed to his "hypostatic vision of the Father."

28. Weinandy, "Jesus' Filial Vision of the Father," 193 (emphasis original).

the Father.[29] The Son sees the Father as he is, that is, as God, and so comes to know himself as God as the Father is God.[30] In humanly perceiving the Father as Father, the Son, in turn, perceives himself as truly Son of the Father.[31] For Weinandy, the self-consciousness of the Son is predicated on this filial insight.[32] Such an image is reflected within the immanent Trinity, whereby the Father and the Son are relationally dependent on one another for their own identities as Father and Son. This is visible from the fact that the Father would not be the Father without the Son. In the same manner, without the Father, the Son would not really be the Son.[33] The Father cannot know himself as the Father apart from the Son, and neither can the Son know himself as the Son apart from the Father.[34] It then follows, Weinandy explains, that, as the identity of the Son as the Son is relationally dependent on the Father as his Father, so too is the human self-consciousness of the Son dependent upon the Son's knowledge of the Father as his Father. He further argues that, within the immanent Trinity, the Son understands himself as the Son not in relation to his own divinity, but rather in accordance with his personal relationship with the Father.[35] Prior

29. Weinandy, "Jesus' Filial Vision of the Father," 193.

30. Weinandy, "Jesus' Filial Vision of the Father," 193.

31. Weinandy, "Jesus' Filial Vision of the Father," 193.

32. Nicholas J. Healy Jr. is of similar mind, stating that: "When the Gospel of John refers to Jesus' knowledge of God, the object of his knowledge is not simply the divine essence but the Person of the Father. In terms of both his self-awareness and his relation to God, Christ's deepest identity is to be the Son of the Father," see Healy, "*Simul viator et comprehensor,*" 349.

33. Weinandy, *Jesus becoming Jesus,* 188, footnote 8.

34. Weinandy, *Jesus becoming Jesus,* 194.

35. Weinandy, "The Beatific Vision and the Incarnate Son," 614.

to his Incarnation, the Son knew himself as *homoousios* with the Father by knowing the Father as his Father. It is in this same manner that the Son, during his earthly life, knows himself as *homoousios* with the Father, in seeing the Father as he is through his human filial vision.[36] This idea is verified by the language employed by the Son in the Gospel accounts. In the Gospel, the Son does not refer to himself as "the divine Son," but instead refers only to his "heavenly Father."[37] In a manner most similar, the Father never proclaims himself to be simply "the Father," but instead, as witnessed especially during the account of Jesus' baptism, reveals himself as the Father only in reference to his Son.[38] It is through revealing the Son that the Father reveals himself as the Father of the Son. In the same way, it is only through his interpersonal relationship with the Father that the Incarnate Son becomes conscious of himself as the divine Son.

As has been demonstrated, Weinandy's attempt at providing an answer for the issue of the Son's self-consciousness follows a trinitarian structure. This is because he places the self-consciousness of the Son in

36. Weinandy, "The Beatific Vision and the Incarnate Son," 614.

37. Weinandy, *Jesus becoming Jesus*, 188, footnote 8.

38. Weinandy, *Jesus becoming Jesus*, 196–97, footnote 19. François Dreyfus, OP, confirms this idea, stating: "If we return to the Gospel . . . there is one thing which is quite striking. Jesus doesn't speak of himself, his own greatness, his own dignity, but only of his relationship with the Father. . . . Jesus does not manifest himself directly as God, but as Son of God, Son of the Eternal Father. . . . This is absolutely essential. Jesus doesn't have an awareness of being God by some sort of reflex consciousness, but through his glance and look of filial love toward his Father. . . . In his look of love toward the Father Jesus sees that the Father has given everything to him . . . and that this total gift is completely reciprocal: 'All I have is yours and all you have is mine,'" see Dreyfus, *Did Jesus Know He Was God?*, 106–7.

the context of the Son's knowledge of the Father, and it is through the Son's knowledge of the Father that the Son, in turn, becomes self-conscious of himself as the Son. In furthering this idea, Weinandy argues that it is through the mediation of the Holy Spirit that the Son possesses this filial vision.[39] This follows the trinitarian doctrine of Weinandy who has previously argued that, within the immanent Trinity, the Holy Spirit conforms the Son to be the loving Son of the Father, while also conforming the Father to be the loving Father of the Son.[40] This inner-trinitarian structure finds expression in the life of the Incarnate Son whereby the Son, through the mediation of the Holy Spirit, experiences a vision of the Father that in turn makes him conscious of his identity as the Son.[41] As the Son became Incarnate by the power of the Holy Spirit, so too does the Son, through the mediation of the Spirit of sonship, come to know himself as the divine Son.[42] In this way, the manner through which the Son possesses his vision is radically different from the conceptions of Maritain and Rahner who both argued that the Son experiences his respective vision as a consequence of the hypostatic union. For these aforementioned authors, it is because the humanity is hypostatically united to the Son that the Son, in his human life and intellect, experiences a vision that informs him of his divine identity. This view, according to Weinandy, corresponds to a Docetic or Monophysite understanding of the Incarnation, where the humanity "runs off the steam" of the divinity.[43] Weinandy argues that rather than

---

39. Weinandy, "Jesus' Filial Vision of the Father," 196–97.

40. Weinandy, *The Father's Spirit of Sonship*, 17.

41. Weinandy, "Jesus' Filial Vision of the Father," 197.

42. Weinandy, "Jesus' Filial Vision of the Father," 196.

43. Weinandy, "Jesus' Filial Vision of the Father," 196.

experiencing a vision as a consequence of the hypostatic union, the Son, through the mediation of the Holy Spirit, sees the Father as his Father and so too, through the Spirit, is conformed to be the loving Son of the Father.[44] This is not only reflected within the inner life of the Trinity but it also becomes a paradigm for all Christian believers who, through the Holy Spirit, receive knowledge of the Father as their own Father and, in turn, come to see themselves as sons and daughters of God.[45] It is through knowing the Father in the Spirit that believers become self-conscious of their own identities as children of God.[46]

Furthermore, it is argued that the Son's filial vision of the Father was not experienced by the Son from the moment of his conception, as had been classically conceived in the case of the beatific vision.[47] Rather, in accordance with St. Luke's statement (Luke 2:52) and with Jesus' role as wayfarer, the filial vision of the Son made man advanced throughout the course of his life, being increased through prayer and through the mediation of the Holy Spirit.[48] Weinandy states:

44. This trinitarian structure of Jesus' self-awareness and knowledge is also reflected in the thoughts of the International Theological Commission: "The life of Jesus testifies to his consciousness of a filial relationship with the Father" and that this "relationship of the incarnate Son with the Father presumes in the first place the mediation of the Holy Spirit, who must therefore be always included in the consciousness of Jesus as Son," see Sharkey, *ITC: Texts and Documents*, 308, 310. The Pontifical Biblical Commission, in its document "The Bible and Christology," also confirms the importance of the Son's identity as rooted in his filial knowledge of the Father, see Murphy, *Church and the Bible*, 1335–36.

45. Weinandy, *The Father's Spirit of Sonship*, 105.

46. Weinandy, *The Father's Spirit of Sonship*, 35.

47. Weinandy, "Jesus' Filial Vision of the Father," 197.

48. Weinandy, "Jesus' Filial Vision of the Father," 197.

III. THOMAS WEINANDY

> As Jesus, as a young boy, studied the Scriptures and prayed the Spirit illuminated his human consciousness and intellect with the vision of the Father such that he became hypostatically aware of the Father's glory and love, and within such an awareness he became conscious of his divine identity and so came to know that he was indeed the Father's eternal and only begotten Son.[49]

In keeping with ordinary human experience and psychology, Jesus became aware of his identity at an age that is common for human persons to recognize their own human identities, except, in the case of Christ, it is a divine person becoming aware that he is divine in a manner that is truly human.[50] This awareness, brought about through the Son's human filial vision of the Father, reaches its culmination at the resurrection where Jesus becomes true

49. Weinandy, "Jesus' Filial Vision of the Father," 197.

50. Weinandy, "Jesus' Filial Vision of the Father," 197, 198, footnote 14. In addressing the moment that Jesus became conscious of his identity as the Son, Weinandy emphasizes the humanity of Jesus and predicates the self-knowledge of the Son as authentically flowing from it. Because Jesus is fully human, and lives, thinks, and articulates himself in an authentic human manner, then the way in which Jesus comes to know his divine identity is within the confines of true human experience, that is, not in conception, but through experience and time. The means by which he realizes this is in relation to his personal vision of the Father. Galot shares a very similar understanding, arguing: "This gradual growth in consciousness developed according to the laws of human psychology. Jesus possessed at the start the consciousness of a child, then the consciousness of an adolescent, and finally the consciousness of an adult. His filial consciousness was enriched by what he learned from the Jewish religion, and especially from the Bible. But the 'key' to this consciousness lay in the filial relationship he developed with the One who gave himself to him in the intimate light of mystical contacts as his real Father," see Galot, *Who is Christ?*, 342.

comprehensor.[51] This coincides well with the Letter to the Hebrews which states that Jesus was made perfect through his death and resurrection (Heb 2:10; 5:9; 7:28; 10:14).[52] In this way, Weinandy believes that his conception of the Son's filial consciousness as predicated on his vision of the Father remains faithful to both the incarnational principles that govern the earthly life of the Son and especially to his role as viator.

Secondary Objects of Knowledge

In seeing the Father through his human filial vision, Jesus perceived also all that the Father willed for him throughout his life, and so was able to fulfill the Father's will perfectly.[53] In regard to whether Jesus knew all those for whom he had died, Weinandy recognizes that this is indeed an important issue, one that he wishes to answer positively.[54] It is thus maintained by Weinandy that the Son as man, through his human filial vision of the Father, possessed also an awareness of the individuals for whom he gave up his life.[55] Weinandy admits, however, that the exact manner of the Son's knowing in this domain remains shrouded in mystery.[56] Despite this, it can nevertheless be

51. Weinandy writes: "As we will only become fully aware of who we really are in heaven, so does the incarnate Son of God become fully aware of who he really is in heaven," see Weinandy, "Jesus' Filial Vision of the Father," 198.

52. Weinandy, "Jesus' Filial Vision of the Father," 198.

53. Weinandy, "Jesus' Filial Vision of the Father," 199.

54. Weinandy, "Jesus' Filial Vision of the Father," 198.

55. Weinandy, "Jesus' Filial Vision of the Father," 199.

56. In a manner similar to those who hold the beatific vision to be non-conceptual, Weinandy argues that the knowledge provided to the Son through his filial vision, including his knowledge of

concluded that Weinandy's notion of the filial vision allows Christians to confidently proclaim, with St. Paul, that the Son knew them and died for them.

In addressing the supposed ignorance of Christ concerning the last day, Weinandy argues that the Son's knowledge of the last day is predicated upon his possession of a human "I." It is said by Weinandy that if the Son lived and acted within his divine transcendence, within the parameters of a divine "I," then the Son, in pleading eschatological ignorance, would be a liar since the Son would have certainly known the "day and hour."[57] However, in his Incarnate state, where the Son lives, acts, and is self-conscious within the confines of his human "I," the Son indeed did not know the "day and hour."[58] This is because the Incarnate Son, although being given all things by the Father, is given only that which pertains to the economy of salvation, and so it is claimed by Weinandy that this knowledge of the last day was not given to the Son during his human life.[59]

Criticisms

Weinandy's notion of the Son's filial vision of the Father is an admirable attempt at explaining how it is that the Incarnate Son is humanly self-conscious of his divine identity in his earthly life. Especially commendable is Weinandy's attempt at predicating the Son's self-consciousness within

---

individual believers for whom he died, may also be non-conceptual and thus inarticulable to a certain degree, see Weinandy, "Jesus' Filial Vision of the Father," 199, footnote 18.

57. Weinandy, "Human 'I' of Jesus," 265.
58. Weinandy, "Human 'I' of Jesus," 265.
59. Weinandy, *Jesus becoming Jesus,* 195, footnote 16.

the framework of incarnational and trinitarian principles. In treating the Son's self-consciousness in light of these governing principles, Weinandy is able to emphasize a real involvement of both the Father and the Holy Spirit in the self-consciousness of the Son, with the Father serving as the object of Christ's vision and the Holy Spirit acting as the mediating principle for the vision. Although Weinandy's theory is laudable in a number of ways, it has nonetheless been met with criticisms from a number of different authors.

One such author is Edward T. Oakes, SJ, who contends that Weinandy's filial vision fails to take into account the distinction between the Son's knowledge of the Father and the Son's self-reflective awareness of who he is as the Son of the Father. For Oakes, it seems that to attribute knowledge of the Father to the Son does not suffice as an account for the Son's immediate knowledge of himself as the Son. Oakes uses Lonergan as an example and states that it was the idea of Lonergan not to speak of the beatific vision, but rather to opt for the term beatific *knowledge* "in order to stress Christ's self-awareness of his identity and mission and not just his awareness of his relationship with the Father."[60] In turn, Oakes argues that it is actually necessary to attribute the beatific vision to the Incarnate Son in order to avoid the Nestorian conundrum. He states that without the immediate knowledge granted to Christ by the beatific vision, "the *what* of what Jesus would be aware of would be a human self, *groping toward* a gradually drawing awareness of something *odd* about his self. . . . But surely the Gospels portray a Jesus far more self-aware and self-assured than that!"[61]

---

60. Oakes, *Infinity Dwindled to Infancy*, 221, footnote 101.

61. Oakes, *Infinity Dwindled to Infancy*, 216 (emphasis original).

Similar criticisms have been made by Simon Francis Gaine, OP, who argues that the filial vision of Weinandy fails as a legitimate alternative to the traditional notion of the beatific vision. Gaine wonders how it is that the Son can have such a knowledge of the Father to the extent that the Son "comes to know the Father as the Father truly exists" without possessing a knowledge of the divine essence "with which the Father is identical?"[62] He further insists that the filial vision is not enough to provide the Son with evidential certitude of his divine identity since it is not an immediate vision as is the beatific vision. To demonstrate the supposed inadequacy of the filial vision, Gaine points to Weinandy's treatment of the development of the Son's vision which occurs in time through the finite means of prayer and the pondering of the Scriptures. Gaine argues that this serves as evidence that the filial vision of Weinandy is not at all an immediate vision, but rather is a kind of indirect knowledge dependent on various finite means for clarity. By this measure, Gaine argues that the filial vision is a rather "unclear" vision that is incapable of rendering in Christ evidential certitude of his divine identity.[63] This would render the earthly Christ's awareness of his divine identity an act of faith rather than one of certain knowledge, a conclusion that Weinandy is careful to avoid.[64]

The final criticism concerns the attempt of Weinandy to judge the subjective psychological experiences of Christ through the means of ordinary human psychology.[65] In

62. Gaine, *Did the Saviour See the Father?*, 123.

63. Gaine, *Did the Saviour See the Father?*, 123.

64. Gaine, *Did the Saviour See the Father?*, 123.

65. I am here referring to Weinandy's statement: "In keeping with ordinary human psychology, the Son became humanly conscious of

regard to such an attempt, Hans Urs von Balthasar once stated that Christ's experience of God must not be judged "by the laws of ordinary human psychology, which cannot grasp the hypostatic union."[66] Although Balthasar was not specifically addressing the work of Weinandy, there is perhaps some validity to his remark. It has often been regarded by theologians and even by the Congregation for the Doctrine of the Faith that ontology precedes psychology.[67] That is, the psychological study of an existent is dependent upon its ontological constitution. Although the authentic human mode of the Son's existence is a point of emphasis for Weinandy, it could be argued that, if it is indeed true that ontology precedes psychology, then the psychological experience of Christ is not entirely analogous to our own by virtue of the fact that the Son's ontological constitution differs from our own. That is, although the Son has assumed true human flesh, which thereby results in a true human mode of expression, to attribute to Christ the same ordinary psychological activity as other human beings may not fully take into account the unique character of the Son's existence. That is to say that although the Son does indeed possess a true human nature, this human nature does not exist and function independent of that to which it is hypostatically united, the divine Son. As Balthasar argues, the Son's unique ontological constitution

---

who he was at the appropriate age," see Weinandy, "Jesus' Filial Vision of the Father," 197.

66. Balthasar, *Seeing the Form*, 328, footnote 141.

67. For the connection between ontology and psychology in the works of theologians, see Galot, *Who is Christ?*, 334; Lonergan, *Ontological and Psychological Constitution of Christ*, 221. For this connection made by the CDF, see its notification *On the Works of Father Jon Sobrino SJ*, sec. 8.

as the divine Son perhaps renders invalid the method of judging the Incarnate Son's psyche through the means of ordinary human psychology.

IV. Final Remarks

THE THESES OF MARITAIN, Rahner, and Weinandy have
provided substantial groundwork for the question at hand.
As maintained by the aforementioned authors, Jesus knew
that he was divine in his human mind through an intellectual vision provided to him during his life. This is a
necessary assertion since human knowledge, being finite
and limited in its essence, cannot attain knowledge of
the divine without the mediation of grace.[1] In the case
of Christ, no amount of self-reflexivity or introspection
is sufficient in enabling him to grasp the knowledge of
his own divine identity. Having reviewed the proposed
solutions of the three foregoing authors, this final section
will aim to elucidate an appropriate conception of the
kind of vision that Jesus possessed. This will, in turn, help
us to provide an answer as to how the Son knew himself
as God within his human mind. In addition to this, the
scope of Jesus' human knowledge, as it especially pertains
to his knowledge of individual believers and his supposed
ignorance of the eschaton, will be explored.

---

1. The Catechism states: "Because of his transcendence, God
cannot be seen as he is, unless he himself opens up his mystery to
man's immediate contemplation and gives him the capacity for it," see
Catechism of the Catholic Church, 1028.

The Filial Vision of Christ

In order to preserve the integrity of the true humanity of Christ as declared at the Council of Chalcedon, it must be said that his vision cannot preclude or impede upon his concrete historical subjectivity. It cannot affect his corporeal-sensate and psychosomatic faculties to the extent that Jesus would no longer act as true man. That is, the vision cannot raise Jesus' human operations to heights that are inexplicably foreign or incompatible with human nature. The vision, in order to be compatible with the Son's true human nature and historical functioning as man, must not render the human action of Jesus as inauthentically human. This means that although the human knowledge of Jesus possessed a universal character which allowed him to communicate the deepest truths about God, the human condition, and salvation, it was nonetheless subject to historical and cultural conditioning while also increasing through true human modes of acquisition.[2] Maintaining both these positions may seem like a contradictory and valueless exercise, one which does harm to the historical agency and voluntary action of Jesus as man. However, the nature of the Incarnation demands that we both recognize and hold in careful balance these two seemingly apparent qualities of Christ. This is where the distinctions in consciousness, as present in the works of Maritain and Rahner, are advantageous. By distinguishing between the different levels of consciousness in the Incarnate Son,

2. White aptly remarks: "If God truly became human, then in his human life, the Word Incarnate not only acquired knowledge but also spoke and thought through the medium of the language and symbols of his epoch, set against the complex Judaic and Hellenistic backdrop that such language and symbols presupposed," see White, "Infused Science of Christ," 622.

we can affirm the universal depth of Christ's knowledge on the one hand and its historical conditioning and purview on the other. Although Maritain's conception of the supraconscious and wayfaring consciousness is a noteworthy attempt to hold these two in order, such a distinction between Christ's psyche as comprehensor and Christ's psyche as wayfarer perhaps borders too far along the lines of a double *ego* in Christ. Conversely, Rahner's distinction between basic and reflexive consciousness is a more nuanced approach that takes into account the idea that objects can be known on different levels and in different ways. By adopting Rahner's account of the distinction between basic and reflexive consciousness, we can account for both the universality and profundity of Christ's knowledge while, at the same time, recognizing that it was subject to both historical conditioning and development over the course of his life.

Although Rahner's distinction between basic and reflexive consciousness is a facet of his work that is useful in approaching the present question, his conception of the vision as Jesus' human soul knowing the Word could be said to possess a Nestorian undertone. This was the chief criticism of Rahner's work, namely, that he had failed to adequately account for the patricentricity of Jesus' knowing. As frequently attested to in the Scriptures, Jesus' knowledge and identity are founded on his relationship with the Father whom he comes to reveal and proclaim. In revealing the Father, the Son reveals himself as the Son of the Father. This point is central to the thesis of Weinandy and it is an idea that certainly needs to be preserved. In his vision, the Son sees the Father in an immediate way such that he comes to know himself as the Son of God.[3]

3. The Catechism states that this historical knowledge of Jesus is also the knowledge of the Word which knows, first and foremost, "the

This can be substantiated by the fact that human beings are relational creatures and learn about themselves in relation to others. Human self-awareness, then, consequently entails relationship with others. Christ is no exception here and his self-awareness necessarily possesses a filial character that manifests itself in relation to another, the Father.[4] This is the way in which the Gospels portray the knowledge of Christ, that is, as totally centered on his Father and not on himself. In light of these considerations, Rahner's conception of Jesus' self-consciousness as occurring through relation to himself, and Maritain's notion of Jesus' self-awareness as predicated on the vision of his own divine essence, fall short.

In the case of the beatific vision, it had been traditionally maintained that the primary object of this vision is the "divine essence."[5] Such language is admittedly am-

---

intimate and immediate knowledge that the Son of God made man has of his Father," see *Catechism of the Catholic Church*, 473.

4. Galot maintains this sentiment, stating: "From this point of view likewise, we can discern the harmonious interrelationship of Jesus' psychology and ontology. Person is defined as a subsistent or hypostatic relation: we have emphasized the relational nature of the person. The Son, a divine person, is defined by his filial relationship. Now, he became humanly conscious of himself through his filial relations with his Father. *It was by becoming aware that he was the Son that Jesus became aware that he was God.* The Father revealed himself to him in very deep mystical contacts that made him grasp his identity as the Son of God" (emphasis original), see Galot, *Who is Christ?*, 342.

5. Aquinas, *Summa Theologica*, IIIa Suppl., q. 92, aa. 1–3. See also Pope Benedict XII in *Benedictus Deus*, by which he states: "Since the Passion and death of the Lord Jesus Christ, these souls have seen and see the divine essence with an intuitive vision and even face to face, without the mediation of any creature by way of object of vision; rather the divine essence immediately manifests itself to them, plainly, clearly, and openly, and in this vision they enjoy the divine essence," see Denzinger et al., *Compendium*, 1000.

biguous and fails to properly take into account the filial relationship between the Father and the Son. In spite of this, it must be admitted here that, since the "divine essence" is not and cannot be ontologically distinct from the trinitarian *hypostases*, there is contained within the beatific vision an element of filiality between the knower and the known. That is to say, if the beatific vision is understood as entailing within its purview the distinct trinitarian persons, then we must concede that the traditional conception of Jesus' beatific vision can indeed provide some account of the filial relationship between the Father and the Son. Notwithstanding this, it is perhaps more exact to nuance Jesus' vision as a filial vision since this conception emphasizes more fully the relational nature of the Son's self-knowledge and is, as will be demonstrated, more appropriate with his function as wayfarer. The filial vision, as proposed by Weinandy, not only accentuates the trinitarian relations that exist between the divine persons but also rightly centers the Son's self-knowledge as dependent upon such relations. It does not, as Gaine has claimed, preclude the knowledge of the divine essence, since in the filial vision, the Son sees the Father "as he truly is," and in seeing the Father "as he truly is," the Son sees not only *who* the Father is as his Father but also *what* the Father is, namely, God. In seeing the Father as he truly exists, the Son sees himself as he truly exists and, in turn, becomes subjectively self-conscious of himself as both true God and as the Son of the Father. Therefore, although the beatific vision is a commendable conception, one that classically helped to safeguard important truths about Christ's identity and his self-knowledge, it seems better to nuance it in the way that Weinandy has done so as to emphasize the filial inter-trinitarian relationships that serve as the foundation for the Son's self-knowledge.

Through his filial vision, the Son does not see God in a comprehensive and all-encompassing manner. It must be noted here that the Son made man, in his human historical mode of functioning, does not know God in the same way and to the same degree that God knows God. This is because, as had been maintained by St. Thomas, the infinite cannot be contained or comprehended in the finite, and so we cannot say that Christ, in his finite mind, knew God comprehensively through his vision.[6] Moreover, in accordance with his identity as wayfarer, the vision of Christ must be said to have increased in the richness of objective content over the course of his life and was perfected at the resurrection.[7] If Jesus possessed the beatific vision from the moment of his conception, then the direct self-communication of God to the human soul of Christ was fully maximized from the moment of his Incarnate existence; that is, it did not increase over the course of his life. More than this, the theory of Jesus' beatific vision implies that he was conscious of his identity from the very moment of his conception. That is to say that Jesus, as a zygote, saw the divine essence in a manner more perfect than all the saints and had knowledge of all truths in act.[8] Such a view seems difficult to reconcile

6. Aquinas, *Summa Theologica*, III, q. 10, a. 1.

7. Here we can include the importance of prayer in the life of the Son. In uniting his heart and mind to the Father in prayer, the Son comes to see the Father in a manner that is continually perfected over the course of his life.

8. Aquinas, *Summa Theologica*, III, q. 7, a. 3; III, q. 10, a. 2; III, q. 34, a. 2, ad. 2; III, q. 34, a. 4. See also Galot, *Who is Christ?*, 359. Gaine confirms this, stating that "Aquinas taught that Christ possessed it [the beatific vision] from the first moment of his conception, and by it saw not only the essence of God but also all that was, is or will be, in any way whatever, done, thought or said by all, at any time," see Gaine, *Did the Saviour See the Father?*, 5. St. Thomas also held

with the role of Jesus as true man and wayfarer.[9] In order to make the concept of the Son's vision more compatible with his authentic human development, it should instead be argued that Jesus, from the moment of his conception, did not possess a perfected direct self-communication of God to his human soul. This is not to say that Jesus did not possess the fullness of the Godhead, nor that the Word, in taking on human flesh, relinquished his divinity and his divine attributes so as to "make way" for his true human existence. Rather, what is being argued here is the understanding that the self-communication of the Father

---

that Christ, from the moment of his conception, could freely will and merit salvation for humanity, see Aquinas, *Summa Theologica,* III, q. 34, aa. 2–3. Weinandy argues that the ability of the embryonic Christ to freely will and merit salvation for us mitigates the soteriological significance of Jesus' human nature, since it treats the embryonic cell as a mere "host" for the agent intellect and will, rather than as an active instrument in the salvation of humanity, see Weinandy, "The Hypostatic Union," 118.

9. Galot states that "Christ's human life began in unconsciousness, just like every other human life, and his consciousness awakened gradually. This process was not accelerated in Jesus, since the Incarnation did not involve any speeding up of the laws of nature," see Galot, *Who is Christ?,* 359. While an interesting notion, we wish to nuance Galot's use of the phrase "consciousness" to a more specific declaration, namely, that Jesus, as an infant, although possessing sensate forms of consciousness, was not intellectually conscious in the rationally discursive sense. That is to say, the Son could not form conceptual judgments about his divinity or about certain truths in act during his infancy, but such intellectual development occurred later in time over the course of his life. As a result of this, the knowledge of the infant Jesus extending to all truths in act seems to carry with it no efficacious result. It is superfluous insofar as such knowledge cannot be communicated to others for the purpose of salvation. This is not to say that Jesus did not possess any special knowledge until the time of his public ministry, but rather that, in accordance with all authentic human existence, Jesus' life began in nescience or "unconsciousness" in Galot's sense, and then awakened gradually.

expressed through filial love in the Spirit was made known to Christ in a progressively perfected manner; and that this view seems to find itself compatible with the declaration of St. Luke ("Jesus increased in wisdom . . . and in favor with God and man"), the kenosis of Christ as portrayed in Phil 2:7 ("but emptied himself, taking the form of a servant"), and the progressive perfection of Jesus achieved through his death and resurrection (Heb 2:10; 5:9; 7:28).[10]

As a consequence of this, Gaine's criticism of the Son's filial vision being an "unclear vision" since it increases over time through the finite means of prayer is inadequate. This is because the progression of the Son's filial vision does not thereby render this vision as unclear or non-immediate, nor does it seem to suggest that Jesus "discovered" something that he did not hitherto know about. Its development, rather, coincides necessarily with the function of Jesus as viator. As a result of this, the Son's filial vision of the Father is not incomprehensible as is the beatific vision since it is not perfected from the moment of the Son's Incarnate existence.[11] With this in mind, there is no need to posit the infused science of Jesus as a necessary "translator" of the vision, as Maritain does, since

10. This point is underscored by Weinandy, who states that "[t]he Incarnation demands that the Word actually became flesh (*sarx*) (see John 1:14), not in some perfect idyllic state, but in a manner that is to be perfected through what he suffers (see Heb 2:10)," see Weinandy, "The Hypostatic Union," 115. The Pontifical Biblical Commission, in similar fashion, writes that Jesus "grows more and more in the awareness of the mission entrusted to him by the Father, from his childhood up to his death on the cross. Finally, he experiences death in as cruel a fashion as any other human would (*cf.* Mt 26:39; 27:46 and par.); or, as the Epistle to the Hebrews puts it, 'Son though he was, he learned obedience from what he suffered' (5:8)," see Murphy, *Church and the Bible*, 1336.

11. Weinandy, "The Hypostatic Union," 122.

the contents of the filial vision were not so non-conceptual that they needed to be "converted" into ideative forms and human lexicon.[12] Instead, the human intellect of Christ, enlightened by the presence of the Holy Spirit, allowed the Son to "make sense" of the vision and express its contents through his normal human modes of apprehension.[13] Finally, the enhancement of the filial vision in accordance with the Son's human growth serves as an appropriate paradigm for Christian believers in the state of way. In a similar manner to Christ, but of course, not to the same degree, the knowledge of Christian believers in relation to God advances over the course of their lives, and it is through knowing God that they, in turn, know themselves as adopted sons and daughters of God. Although Jesus enjoys a unique and immediate knowledge of the Father that is unknown in the experience of wayfaring Christians, propounding a progression in the Son's vision of the Father and, in turn, his self-knowledge corresponds well with his function as true man, viator, and as the pioneer and perfecter of our faith (Heb 12:2).

In terms of how Christ comes to possess this vision, it is best to factor in here the involvement of the Holy Spirit within the question of the Son's self-consciousness. Maritain argues that the Son as man possessed his vision as a consequence of the hypostatic union. It is because of the united proximity of the human nature to the divinity that the humanity of Jesus is endowed with perfect attributes pertinent to one who is comprehensor. Such a viewpoint begins with the person of the Word and predicates his vision

---

12. Weinandy, "The Hypostatic Union," 122.
13. Weinandy, "The Hypostatic Union," 122.

as stemming from his transcendence as God.[14] Although an interesting conception, this idea ultimately fails to take into account the Son's self-knowledge as always intimately related to the other trinitarian persons. It is more fitting, then, to render the Holy Spirit as the mediating principle of the Son's filial vision of the Father. This factors in well the involvement of the Spirit in the Son's self-knowledge and leaves a trinitarian imprint on the whole question of his self-consciousness.

Finally, the filial vision should not be conceived as an object present in the mind of Christ which obscures and detracts the attention of Jesus away from the carrying out of his daily activities. This is the immediate connotation that the term "vision" carries, whereby "vision" is conceived as a picture or map which places before the mind of Christ objects in sequential order. The filial vision instead must be understood as immediate and intuitive. It does not occur in fragmented forms, but rather is present to the mind of Christ all at once.[15] The filial vision allows Christ to grasp his Father as God and, in turn, his own divinity as the Son of God in one global act.[16] The qualification of the vision in this way helps to delineate how it is that Christ can possess a filial vision that does not at all impede upon his normal sensitive operations as man.

14. This so-called "principle of perfection" has been criticized by Galot, who has asserted that this line of reasoning lacks sufficient biblical and patristic foundation and is instead founded on *a priori* metaphysical deduction, see Galot, "Le Christ terrestre," 431–32, quoted in White, "Voluntary Action of the Earthly Christ," 501.

15. Wilkins, "Love and Knowledge of God," 87.

16. Moloney, *Knowledge of Christ,* 60.

IV. Final Remarks

Secondary Objects of Knowledge

Before addressing the Son's supposed ignorance of the eschatological time and date and whether the Son knew those for whom he was dying, it is first necessary to situate Christ's human knowledge into its appropriate context. For patristic theologians, the incarnational act was one of salvific value. Indeed, the redemption of human nature was the reason that the Word became flesh. In his battles against Apollinaris, St. Gregory of Nazianzus defended the true humanity of Christ by interpreting it through the lens of soteriology. In assuming true human nature, the Son was able to redeem human nature. For St. Gregory, the human nature of Christ stood as the instrumental cause of our own salvation, and thus he emphatically proclaimed, "that which He has not assumed He has not healed."[17] In the age of the scholastics, St. Thomas developed a treatise on the human knowledge of Christ which never disassociated his human knowledge from its larger soteriological meaning. Concerning the beatific vision, St. Thomas argued that Jesus possessed the beatific vision pre-eminently since he came to give us that which he already possessed, and the cause is always more potent than the effect.[18] To follow suit, any treatment of the human knowledge of Christ in the modern age cannot be severed from the backdrop of soteriology. This sentiment was recognized by Balthasar who also argued that any special knowledge possessed by the Son was always connected to his mission.[19] It is understood, then, that the nature of Jesus' human knowledge serves a soteriological function.

17. Schaff, *Nicene and Post-Nicene Fathers,* 440.
18. Aquinas, *Summa Theologica,* III, q. 9, a. 2, co.
19. Balthasar, *Dramatis Personae: Persons in Christ,* 173.

It has utility insofar as it is used to proclaim the kingdom of God. Theological considerations made about the human knowledge of Christ must better help to elucidate his saving mission, and his saving mission, in turn, must provide appropriate illumination for the mystery of his human knowledge. In this way, the mission of Christ stands as the interpretive key by which to understand the scope of his human knowledge. It is the *mise en scène* for all subsequent considerations on the knowledge and action of Jesus as man. This methodology, therefore, presupposes that, although the human knowledge of the Son had a universal character which transcended the borders of his historical age and culture, it was always intimately related to his mission and so was not superfluously possessed.[20]

With this context in mind, we can make sense of the ignorance of Christ with respect to the eschaton. Given the controversial nature of these texts (Mark 13:32; Matt 24:36), it is safe to assume that these words were *ipsissima verba Christi*. Furthermore, it seems problematic to interpret these passages in such a way that claims that Jesus did indeed know the final "day and hour" but did not wish to reveal it.[21] If this were truly the case, then one wonders

20. The Son as man, for example, while possessing knowledge about the deepest truths of the human condition and the salvific will of God, could not communicate at the same time geometrical truths or a comprehensive understanding of pyrotechnics, since such knowledge would have been inessential to his mission. Weinandy expresses similar convictions in Weinandy, "The Hypostatic Union," 115–16, footnote 31.

21. Such a solution was implemented by some of the early Church Fathers and continued to bear life even during the period of the scholastic theologians, see Aquinas, *Summa Theologica,* III, q. 10, a. 2, obj. 1, ad. 1. As Christoph Schönborn argues, "the attempt by most Church Fathers to gloss over the ignorance of Jesus is unsatisfactory. They interpret all the texts that suggest Jesus' ignorance pedagogically. . . . The statement of Jesus that even the Son does not know the hour when the world will

why Jesus did not articulate his words in a manner similar to his statement in Acts 1:7, where he states: "It is not for you to know times or seasons which the Father has fixed by his own authority." Instead, the Son made man attributes exclusive knowledge about the eschaton to the Father alone ("nor the Son, but the Father only"). In light of our previous considerations about the scope of Jesus' human knowledge being intimately tied to his soteriological mission, we can affirm ignorance in the Son without rendering harm to his identity as true Lord. Here we wish to make a distinction between the divine knowledge of the Son by which he knows all things and his human knowledge which is both exercised in history and subject to limitation.[22] In the divine mind, the Son certainly knows all that the Father knows. However, during his life on earth, the Son as man knew only that which the Father chose to reveal to him for the purpose of his saving mission. Since this knowledge of the day of judgment contains no soteriological utility, it was not necessary that the Son as man, in his human finite mind, should possess such ineffectual insight.

In regard to whether the Son as man knew those for whom he was dying, this question should be answered in the affirmative. Through his filial vision of the Father, which revealed to the Son his personal intimate union with the Father, the Son saw also those personally united

---

end (Mk 13:32) is interpreted to the effect that Jesus did in fact know the hour but did not wish to reveal it," see Schönborn, *God Sent His Son,* 167.

22. Galot's remarks are helpful in unpacking the historical implications of the dyophysitism of Christ, especially as it pertains to the functioning of the Incarnate Word through his assumed human nature. He states: "The divine person of the Word, in operating through the [human] nature, does not modify the laws of this nature's behavior. The Word respects the human nature and conforms to all of its limitations," see Galot, *Who is Christ?,* 335.

to him in a mysterious and incomprehensible way.[23] That is to say, the Son was endowed not only with filial insight into the trinitarian persons to which he was ontologically united but also with an insight into those that were filially united to him through his saving will.[24] This awareness of particular persons was not foreign to Christ who, during his life, had often shown the ability to penetrate the innermost thoughts of human hearts (Mark 2:8; Matt 9:4; 12:25; Luke 5:22; 9:47; 11:14–17; John 13:11; 13:27). We should not be irresolute, then, to affirm that the Son possessed an intimate knowledge of individuals in a similar manner while on the cross. Furthermore, it is necessary to note that this knowledge of individual persons contains real soteriological purpose. In fact, it can be argued that it is integral to Christ's mission. This is because the Son's mission of redemption is carried out in a personal and intimate way. It necessarily entails a personal love and knowledge for each individual sheep (John 10:14).[25] Jesus

23. The International Theological Commission states that "this love has not been understood by the Church as just a general attitude but as a concrete love expressed in terms of personal consideration for every individual," see Sharkey, *ITC: Texts and Documents,* 314. William Brownsberger makes a similar statement: "The Christ of Galatians did not redeem Paul because Paul happened to have the ticket of being human. He did not redeem Paul because Paul was the member of a class of beings that Christ generically pictured in connection with his sacrificial action and that he took with himself to the Cross. He loved Paul as Paul," see Brownsberger, *Jesus the Mediator,* 70.

24. This knowledge is not bound by time or space but is universal in its depth. Pius XII affirms that, through his vision of God, all the members of the Church were present to Christ in an intimate and boundless manner, see Pius XII, *Mystici Corporis Christi,* 75.

25. Brownsberger aptly comments that "[w]hile we have to be on guard against prooftexting Jesus' indications in Jn 10 that he knows his sheep intimately, even by name, there is no harm in admitting that

does not save us in mechanical fashion. He takes on the sin of mankind in a personal way because he regards as important the life and dignity of each individual sheep. An act completed in a personal and conscious way is an act done in love. An act completed without these essential elements is a mere dispensation.[26]

It must be noted that the precise manner of his knowing is, for the most part, a mystery. It seems that, on the one hand, such an insight into all individuals, past, present, and future, finds tension with the limitations that are characteristic of any true human mind. On the other hand, such insight is necessary for the *personal* work of Christ's redemption. In attempting to resolve this paradox, Rahner's insight on the distinction between basic and reflexive consciousness could be adopted. In his basic consciousness, the Son knows the individuals for whom he is dying in an immediate and non-expressive way; he knows it within the very depths of his being. However, in his reflexive consciousness, Christ's concrete expression of such mystical knowledge was neither necessary nor fully possible. It is

---

these verses point to the intimate and personal love that Christ, even on earth, bears for his own," see Brownsberger, *Jesus the Mediator*, 71. The soteriological importance of Christ possessing knowledge of each individual believer is highlighted by Matthew Levering in this way: "By possessing the fullness of knowing and loving, he [Christ] is able to *know* each person in light of God's plan for the salvation of all, and he is able to *love* each person who is included in God's plan for the salvation of all. Thus he does not need to wait to meet us in heaven before knowing and loving us; his personal love for each of us is given, in St. Paul's phrase, while we are still in our sins. In short, Christ's establishment in beatitude, far from making him an ahistorical figure, actually enables him, precisely in his historical life, to perform the historical work of salvation in the personal way that it must be performed" (emphasis original), see Levering, *Christ's Fulfillment of Torah and Temple*, 39–40.

26. Brownsberger, *Jesus the Mediator*, 71.

important to note that the limitation which presents itself to the intellect of Christ here is one of expression and not of knowledge. That is to say, the Son knows the individuals for whom he gives his life, but the manner in which he knows them is non-conceptual and immediate; they are known only to him in intimate and incommunicable fashion. In this way, it should be maintained that the Son as man knew the men and women for whom he was dying in a personal, immediate, and truly unfathomable way, to the extent that believers can proclaim with St. Paul that the Son "loved me and gave himself for me" (Gal 2:20).[27]

27. This affirmation of the Son's personal knowledge for individual believers bears important relevance for the spirituality of the Church and for the faith and devotion of everyday Catholics. As Healy notes: "What would Jesus' death and Resurrection mean if he did not know for whom he was giving up his life? Our hope for eternal salvation hinges on our being able to confess with Paul that 'the Son of God loved me and gave himself up for me' (Gal 2:20)," see Healy, "*Simul viator et comprehensor*," 345. In addition to this, Schönborn notes that "Paul, and the primitive Church before him, believed Jesus' mission to be of universal significance and breadth. How far can we—must we, may we—assume a thematic consciousness of this breadth? What does '*pro me*' or '*pro nobis*' mean? The great figures in the history of salvation, from Paul to Thérèse of Lisieux (d. 1897), have understood this '*pro me*' in such a concrete sense that they lived from a sure faith that Jesus 'loved *me* and gave himself up for *me*'" (emphasis original), see Schönborn, *God Sent His Son*, 176.

Conclusion

THE CLASSICAL CATHOLIC THEOLOGICAL position held that Jesus knew himself as divine in his human mind through the grace of the beatific vision. Jacques Maritain is an example of an author who maintained this traditional position and helped to develop it further. In recent years, however, emphases on the humanity and the historical subjectivity of Christ have surfaced and have moved theologians to consider this question differently. Karl Rahner and Thomas Weinandy have made attempts to preserve the idea that the Son possessed an intellectual vision of God throughout his life, although their conceptions of Jesus' vision ultimately run on different trains of thought. It has been argued in the final section of this thesis that the nature of Jesus' vision is heavily patricentric and pneumatological. That is, the content of the Son's vision is centered on the Father himself and revealed through the mediation of the Holy Spirit. Moreover, in accordance with his identity as wayfarer, Jesus comes to know the Father in an increasingly progressive and perfected manner, a conclusion that could not be admitted in the case of the beatific vision. Therefore, it seems both appropriate and necessary to nuance the idea of the beatific vision in the way that Weinandy has done so as to emphasize both the filial character of the Son's self-knowledge in relation to the Father and the Spirit, as well as its development over the course of his life.

It has also been argued that Jesus' human knowledge extends only insofar as it is relevant to his saving mission. In first establishing that the knowledge of the eschaton contains no soteriological function, it is appropriate then to deny that Jesus possessed such knowledge in his human mind, as presented in the Gospel accounts. It has also been maintained that there is real soteriological utility in Jesus knowing the individuals for whom he was dying. This is because the Son's mission is carried out in a personal way, and so it is only through the Son's intimate knowledge of individual persons that he is able to redeem them as individual persons and not merely as beings who fall under the general category of "human."

It was the aim of this paper to lay out the historical understandings and the contemporary viewpoints that surround the question of how Jesus knew himself as God in his human mind. More than this, an attempt was made at advancing an answer about the nature of the Son's filial vision which would run in accordance with Scripture, Tradition, and the dogmatic pronouncements concerning the ontological constitution of the Son of God made man, especially with his role as wayfarer. By this, it is hoped that this thesis has provided some contribution to the present issue and helped to direct it towards a more precise future answer.

Bibliography

Aquinas, Thomas. *Summa Theologica*. Translated by Fathers of the English Dominican Province. New York: Benziger Brothers, 1947.

Ashley, Benedict M. "The Extent of Jesus' Human Knowledge according to the Fourth Gospel." In *Reading John with St. Thomas Aquinas: Theological Exegesis and Speculative Theology*, edited by Michael Dauphinais and Matthew Levering, 241–53. Washington, DC: Catholic University of America Press, 2005.

Ashton, John. "The Consciousness of Christ I." *The Way* 10, no. 1 (1970) 59–71.

Balthasar, Hans Urs von. *Dramatis Personae: Persons in Christ*. Vol. III of *Theo-Drama: Theological Dramatic Theory*. Translated by Graham Harrison. San Francisco: Ignatius, 1992.

———. *Seeing the Form*. Vol. 1 of *The Glory of the Lord: A Theological Aesthetics*. Translated by Erasmo Leiva-Merikakis and edited by Joseph Fessio and John Riches. Edinburgh: T. & T. Clark, 1982.

———. *You Crown the Year with Your Goodness: Radio Sermons*. Translated by Graham Harrison. San Francisco: Ignatius, 1989.

Brownsberger, William L. *Jesus the Mediator*. Washington, DC: Catholic University of America Press, 2012.

Catechism of the Catholic Church. 2nd ed. Strathfield: St. Pauls, 1997.

Cessario, Romanus. "Incarnate Wisdom and the Immediacy of Christ's Salvific Knowledge." *Studi Tomistici* 44, no. 5 (1991) 334–40.

Congregation for the Doctrine of the Faith. *On the Works of Father Jon Sobrino SJ*. Notification. Vatican website. November 26, 2006. http://www.vatican.va/roman_curia/congregations/cfaith /documents/rc_con_cfaith_doc_20061126_notification-sobrino_en.html.

de la Taille, M. "Created Actuation by Uncreated Act: Light of Glory, Sanctifying Grace, Hypostatic Union." In *The Hypostatic Union and Created Actuation by Uncreated Act*. Translated by Cyril Vollert. Indiana: West Baden College, 1952.

Denzinger, Heinrich, et al. *Compendium of Creeds, Definitions, and Declarations on Matters of Faith and Morals*. 43rd ed. San Francisco: Ignatius, 2012.

Donnelly, Malachi J. "The Theory of R. P. Maurice De La Taille, S.J. on the Hypostatic Union." *Theological Studies* 2, no. 4 (1941) 510–26.

Dreyfus, Françios. *Did Jesus Know He Was God?*. Translated by Msgr. Michael J. Wrenn. Chicago: Franciscan Herald, 1989.

Dupuis, Jacques. *Who Do You Say I Am? Introduction to Christology*. New York: Orbis, 1994.

Gaine, Simon Francis. *Did the Saviour See the Father? Christ, Salvation and the Vision of God*. London: T. & T. Clark, 2015.

Galot, Jean. *Who is Christ? A Theology of the Incarnation*. Translated by M. Angeline Bouchard. Chicago: Franciscan Herald, 1980.

Garrigou-Lagrange, Reginald. *Our Saviour and His Love for Us*. Translated by A. Bouchard. St. Louis: B. Herder, 1958.

Gutwenger, Engelbert. "The Problem of Christ's Knowledge." In *Who is Jesus of Nazareth?*, translated by Theodore Westow and edited by Edward Schillebeeckx and Boniface Willems, 91–105. New York: Paulist, 1966.

Healy Jr., Nicholas J. "*Simul viator et comprehensor:* The Filial Mode of Christ's Knowledge." *Nova et Vetera* 11, no. 2 (2013) 341–55.

John Paul II. *Novo Millennio Ineunte*. Encyclical Letter. Vatican website. January 6, 2001. http://w2.vatican.va/content/john-paul-ii/en/apost_letters/2001/documents/hf_jp-ii_apl_20010106_novo-millennio-ineunte.html.

Kasper, Walter. *Jesus the Christ*. Translated by V. Green. London: Burns & Oates, 1977.

Leeming, Bernard. "The Human Knowledge of Christ." *Irish Theological Quarterly* 19, no. 3 (1952) 234–53.

Levering, Matthew. *Christ's Fulfillment of Torah and Temple: Salvation According to Thomas Aquinas*. Notre Dame: University of Notre Dame Press, 2002.

Lonergan, Bernard. *The Incarnate Word*. Collected Works of Bernard Lonergan. Translated by Charles C. Hefling Jr. and edited by Robert M. Doran and Jeremy D. Wilkins. Toronto: University of Toronto Press, 2016.

———. *The Ontological and Psychological Constitution of Christ.* Collected Works of Bernard Lonergan. Translated by Michael G. Shields. Toronto: University of Toronto Press, 2002.

Madigan, Kevin. "Did Jesus 'Progress in Wisdom'? Thomas Aquinas on Luke 2:52 in Ancient and High-Medieval Context." *Traditio* 52 (1997) 179–200.

Mansini, Guy. "Understanding St. Thomas on Christ's Immediate Knowledge of God." *The Thomist: A Speculative Quarterly Review* 59, no. 1 (1995) 91–124.

Maritain, Jacques. *On the Grace and Humanity of Jesus.* Translated by Joseph W. Evans. New York: Herder and Herder, 1969.

McDermott, John M. "How Did Jesus Know He Was God? The Ontological Psychology of Mark 10:17–22." *Irish Theological Quarterly* 74, no. 3 (2009) 272–97.

Moloney, Raymond. *The Knowledge of Christ.* London: Continuum, 1999.

———. "The Mind of Christ in Transcendental Theology: Rahner, Lonergan and Crowe." *Heythrop Journal* 25, no. 3 (1984) 288–300.

Murphy, Dennis J. *The Church and the Bible: Official Documents of the Catholic Church.* 2nd ed. New York: St. Pauls, 2007.

Oakes, Edward T. *Infinity Dwindled to Infancy: A Catholic and Evangelical Christology.* Grand Rapids, MI: Eerdmans, 2011.

O'Collins, Gerald. *Christology: A Biblical, Historical, and Systematic Study of Jesus.* Oxford: Oxford University Press, 1995.

O'Collins, Gerald, and Daniel Kendall. "The Faith of Jesus." *Theological Studies* 53, no. 3 (1992) 403–23.

Ormerod, Neil. "Doing the Will of the Father: Jesus' Freedom and the Beatific Vision." *Irish Theological Quarterly* 83, no. 3 (2018) 203–16.

Ott, Ludwig. *Fundamentals of Catholic Dogma.* Translated by Patrick Lynch and edited by James Canon Bastible. Cork: Mercier, 1957.

Pannenberg, Wolfhart. *Jesus—God and Man.* Translated by Lewis L. Wilkins and Duane A. Priebe. London: SCM, 1968.

Patrologiae cursus completus. Series Latina (PL) 217 vols. Edited by J. -P. Migne. Paris, 1844–55.

Pitstick, Alyssa Lyra. *Light in Darkness: Hans Urs von Balthasar and the Catholic Doctrine of Christ's Descent into Hell.* Grand Rapids, MI: Eerdmans, 2007.

Pius XII. *Haurietis Aquas.* Encyclical Letter. Vatican website. May 15, 1956. http://w2.vatican.va/content/pius-xii/en/encyclicals/documents/hf_p-xii_enc_15051956_haurietis-aquas.html.

———. *Mystici Corporis Christi*. Encyclical Letter. Vatican website. June 29, 1943. http://w2.vatican.va/content/pius-xii/en/encyclicals /documents/hf_p-xii_enc_29061943_mystici-corporis-christi. html.

Rahner, Karl. "Christology Today." In *Theological Investigations*, vol. 21. Translated by Hugh M. Riley. London: Darton, Longman & Todd, 1988.

———. "Current Problems in Christology." In *Theological Investigations*, vol. 1. Translated by Cornelius Ernst. London: Darton, Longman & Todd, 1961.

———. "Dogmatic Reflections on the Knowledge and Self-Consciousness of Christ." In *Theological Investigations*, vol. 5. Translated by Karl-H. Kruger. London: Darton, Longman & Todd, 1966.

———. *Foundations of Christian Faith*. Translated by William V. Dych. London: Darton, Longman & Todd, 1978.

Schaff, Philip. *Nicene and Post-Nicene Fathers: Second Series, Volume VII—Cyril of Jerusalem, Gregory of Nazianzen*. Grand Rapids, MI: Eerdmans, 1978.

Schönborn, Christoph Cardinal. *God Sent His Son: A Contemporary Christology*. Translated by Henry Taylor. San Francisco: Ignatius, 2010.

Sharkey, Michael. *International Theological Commission: Texts and Documents, 1969–1985*. San Francisco: Ignatius, 1989.

Weinandy, Thomas G. "The Beatific Vision and the Incarnate Son: Furthering the Discussion." *The Thomist: A Speculative Quarterly Review* 70, no. 4 (2006) 605–15.

———. *Does God Change? The Word's Becoming in the Incarnation*. Petersham, MA: St. Bede's, 1985.

———. *The Father's Spirit of Sonship: Reconceiving the Trinity*. Edinburgh: T. & T. Clark, 1995.

———. "The Human 'I' of Jesus." *Irish Theological Quarterly* 62, no. 4 (1996) 259–68.

———. "The Hypostatic Union: Personhood, Consciousness, and Knowledge." *Nova et Vetera* 17, no. 2 (2019) 103–25.

———. *In the Likeness of Sinful Flesh: An Essay on the Humanity of Christ*. Edinburgh: T. & T. Clark, 1993.

———. *Jesus becoming Jesus: A Theological Interpretation of the Synoptic Gospels*. Washington, DC: Catholic University of America Press, 2018.

———. "Jesus' Filial Vision of the Father." *Pro Ecclesia* 13, no. 2 (2004) 189–201.

White, Thomas Joseph. "Dyotheletism and the Instrumental Human Consciousness of Jesus." *Pro Ecclesia* 17, no. 4 (2008) 396–422.

———. "The Infused Science of Christ." *Nova et Vetera* 16, no. 2 (2018) 617–41.

———. "Jesus' Cry on the Cross and His Beatific Vision." *Nova et Vetera* 5, no. 3 (2007) 555–82.

———. "The Voluntary Action of the Earthly Christ and the Necessity of the Beatific Vision." *The Thomist: A Speculative Quarterly Review* 69, no. 4 (2005) 497–534.

Wilkins, Jeremy. "Love and Knowledge of God in the Human Life of Christ." *Pro Ecclesia* 21, no. 1 (2012) 77–99.

Bibliography

BIBLIOGRAPHY

How Did Jesus Know He Was God?

"William Chami, in his short monograph, has addressed an important and fascinating theological issue—that of how Jesus, as the incarnate Son of God, came to know, in a human manner, that he is the Father's Son. In examining three authors, of whom I am honored to be one of those selected, Chami has placed all of the issues in their historical context, as well as within their contemporary theological setting—and he has done so with meticulous clarity, intellectual creativity, and discriminate judgment. This book is a must-read for anyone addressing the topic of Christ's human consciousness and knowledge."

—Thomas G. Weinandy, OFM Cap., former member of the Vatican's International Theological Commission

"This work should be mandatory reading in every Christology subject. It tackles one of those thorny issues in fundamental theology many would like to avoid, and it does so in a way that makes for easy and exciting reading. One does not have to plough through impenetrable academic jargon. The author can write with clarity without oversimplifying the complexities. It would make a great present for seminarians and other students of theology."

—Tracey Rowland, St. John Paul II Chair of Theology, University of Notre Dame Australia

"In this great little book William Chami presents the position of three prominent theologians on an important and highly debatable issue in contemporary Christology. Chami not only presents the three stances on the self-consciousness of Christ in a fair and impartial manner, but also carries out an informed and intelligent academic evaluation of them. A great contribution from an emerging, promising scholar."

—Mariusz Biliniewicz, Associate Dean, Chair of School Research Committee, and Senior Lecturer in Theology, University of Notre Dame Australia

"After a long period of relative consensus that Jesus humanly enjoyed the beatific vision of God, the general question of the nature of Jesus' human knowledge, and the explicit question of whether or not Jesus knew himself as God with his human mind, are once more 'live' questions. Through his analysis and critique of the arguments of three great scholars, Maritain, Rahner, and Weinandy, Chami makes a valuable contribution to the current debate."

—PETER JOHN MCGREGOR, Lecturer in Theology, Catholic Institute of Sydney

www.ingramcontent.com/pod-product-compliance
Lightning Source LLC
Chambersburg PA
CBHW070512090426
42735CB00012B/2756